ADDICTION MEETS THE LAW OF ATTRACTION

12 STEPS TO CREATING A HAPPY, CLEAN, AND SOBER LIFE

Also by April Aimee Adams:

That Don't Make Ya Bad: A Memoir of Addiction

The Law of Attraction in Action:
Five Steps to Making the Law of Attraction Work for You

Addiction Meets the Law of Attraction

12 Steps to Creating a Happy, Clean, and Sober Life

April Aimee Adams

RODNEE BOOKS, LLC
P.O. Box 750695
Las Vegas, NV 89136
aaaworkshops@gmail.com

ISBN: 9780997505344

Published by Rodnee Books, LLC
P.O. Box 750695
Las Vegas, NV 89136
Email: aaaworkshops@gmail.com

To learn about workshops conducted in conjunction with this book, please visit aaaworkshops.com

For Anyone with an Addiction.

ACKNOWLEDGMENTS

I would like to thank the following people who helped me and/or supported me along the way:

Mom – Thank you for your unconditional love, support, and help.

Brandon and Tiffany – You are the lights in my life…the two most special kids on the planet…and I'm not partial. I love you more than life.

Rhys – You da bomb diggity.

Rand – Thank you for offering love and support as I struggled to finish this book. I'm so grateful to have you in my life.

Belinda – You are the reason I started writing! Thank you for the love, support, and wisdom over the years and for the hope and inspiration to write.

Julie – You will always be one of my dearest friends even though we go long periods of time without seeing each other…years even…let's do lunch.

Theia – Thank you for taking the time to offer your wisdom on the subject of addiction. You have such a sparkling and happy personality! You are very inspiring to me.

Dean – Thank you for knocking thousands of unnecessary words out of the monstrous manuscripts I offer you! You have a knack for turning my jumbled words into easy to understand text.

Monk and Bobby – Thank you for being there for me. I cherish our friendships. Bobby, RIP. See you on the other side.

CONTENTS

HOW TO USE THIS BOOK

Remember Magnum PI, the show with the good-looking private investigator who solved crimes? Like any good investigator, you too must hunt for clues to solve challenges in your life. This book will help provide the clues you need to make your life better. Some of these clues will help tremendously; others may lead to a dead end. Either way, the journey you are about to take will be a learning experience and will make your time on this planet more joyful and fulfilling.

This self-help book is unlike most others. Since there is no "one-size-fits-all" remedy for everyone, I've integrated many techniques that helped me personally. When a certain piece of advice resonates with you, run with it. Write it down on a piece of paper and tape it to your mirror, or put a copy in your pocket. Writing things down not only helps organize information, it reinforces ideas in your mind which helps reinforce your intentions. This is vital since an intention is a creative force that is an essential building block in the creation of our reality. Just by reading this book you're making your intentions known to the universe.

There are also workshops at the end of each section which, if you're left-brained, you'll be tempted to skip and jump to the next section. I understand that thinking, but I strongly urge you to take the time necessary to complete each workshop item. Getting ideas out of your head and putting them into action will add a major dimension to your recovery and the creation of your new reality. Reading this book and completing the workshop items can diminish your need for any addictive substance or behavior and increase your chances of leading a happy, fulfilled life.

In this book, I have used the term "addiction" in the broadest possible sense. It refers to all types of addictions, including alcohol, drugs, sex, shopping, processed foods, or anything else.

I've used the term "addict" as anyone who is addicted to anything, including alcohol.

PREFACE

The gods must be crazy.
Think about it. Was there ever a time when you thought about doing something insane…and the gods said you couldn't? Herein lies the problem. We're free to roam the planet willy-nilly, doing anything we please. For those of us with addictive personalities, that can bring complete and utter disaster. **I'm an alcoholic.** I began drinking when I was 12. I had a DUI when I was 17 and was sent to juvenile hall for a week. I had one-night stands, I was raped by two men, and I lost a job I enjoyed because I was drunk at work. I crashed my Toyota into a fence and hit a gas pump with my classic '72 Chevy convertible after passing out at the wheel. I experienced black-outs on a regular basis. If you've ever blacked-out, you know how frightening it is to have hours of your life wiped from your memory. Often, I only learned later what happened to me from the people I'd been drinking with.

I've even been admitted to the hospital on multiple occasions because of my drinking. I attended a toga party and got so drunk I fell in the bathroom. When I opened the door, everyone gasped. There was blood dripping from my ear all over the pink toga I'd crafted from a sheet. I needed eleven stitches. Another time I found myself in the hospital with no memory of how I'd gotten there. I only knew I was half-naked and had a catheter. Later I learned my blood alcohol level was .40—so high it could have been deadly. My third hospital experience was a déjà vu. I woke up—again half-naked—with no memory of how I'd gotten there and again with a blood alcohol level of .40.

I'm a drug addict. During my teens, I noticed a debilitating lack of energy. I trudged through each day as if walking through quicksand. At any time during the day, I felt like grabbing a pillow, lying on the floor, and falling asleep for hours. I over-ate on a regular basis and couldn't understand how people could skip meals or leave food on their plates. I was ravenous every waking moment.

Methamphetamines were the answer to my prayers. They did the impossible. They suppressed my appetite and provided a boost of energy. With my magic powder, I was Superwoman! I could accomplish anything! Even though it triggered extreme paranoia and sleep deprivation, meth was easier than eating right and exercising. It produced huge pimples on my face and made me look excessively haggard, but that didn't matter. I couldn't get enough of it.

I'm a processed food addict and bulimic. Binge eating and purging was a daily occurrence after I stopped drinking and doing meth. In order to keep my secret, I waited until everyone went to bed. Then I ate until my stomach hurt, devouring thousands of calories at one sitting. When I felt I couldn't eat another bite, I pressed on my stomach until the contents were forcefully ejected into the toilet. After purging, my face was red from bending over. My eyes were bloodshot and vomit dripped from my nose and mouth. No matter how repulsed I felt about my actions, I engaged in the same routine day after day.

Does any of this sound sane to you? To avoid feeling pain of any kind, I always chose the path of least resistance. It seemed easier to endure the insanity of my addictions and experience instant gratification than it was to deal with my fears and insecurities. Food, drugs, and alcohol consumed my thoughts and instigated mind-blowing insanity. Addictions ruled my life for decades, yet I felt powerless to do anything about them. But finally, I decided I couldn't take it anymore. I reached the point where it became necessary to change. Recovering from addiction is not an easy process, but with the right tools and timing—it is possible.

I've written this book to share with you what I learned about addiction recovery. My goal is to help you stay clean and sober, heal emotional issues that may have helped perpetuate your addictions, and show you how to create the life of your dreams. I believe the best way to prevent relapse is to work on self-healing and create a reality which will be more exciting and fulfilling than your addiction ever could be.

PART I
DISCOVER THE TREASURE
OF SOBRIETY

Long johns keep us warm at night, but what keeps us warm during the day? Some find warmth and comfort in their spouses. Others find it in their children or jobs. But others feel empty inside and can't find comfort in anything or anyone. That's where addictive substances and behaviors come in. Engaging in addictions helps people forget they're lonely or sad, or that they carry the weight of the world on their shoulders. It brings fleeting happiness by providing a pleasant, temporary experience.

Unfortunately, giving in to our addictions only leads to pain and sorrow. As addicts, we only concentrate on what makes us feel good *now*. The bigger picture escapes us and we deny our addictions are actually doing us harm. We hang around others who are just as sick as we are, and engage in activities that bring us guilt and shame. Then, predictably, we again turn to our addictions to cover up those shameful feelings and give us a temporary sense of euphoria. . It's a vicious cycle and one that's very difficult to break. Only after overcoming denial and recognizing the signs of addiction, can the process begin. The signs include obsession, lack of control, and negative consequences. These three signs are coupled with the inability to stop using our drug of choice no matter how hard we try.

Recovery from any addiction can be tricky, but it can also be joyous. You must accomplish certain things and break old habits, but you should view recovery as a second chance at life. The ultimate rewards are knowing your true self, loving yourself, and letting go of what doesn't serve you.

✓ Giving into your addictions leads to pain and sorrow.

✓ The signs of addiction include obsession, lack of control, and negative consequences.

✓ Recovery from addiction can be tricky, but it can also be joyous.

✓ You should view recovery as a second chance at life.

✓ The ultimate rewards of recovery are knowing your true self, loving yourself, and letting go of what doesn't serve you.

✓ Recovery permits you to be the best you can be and lead a happy, fulfilling life.

STEP ONE - FLIP THE SWITCH OF DENIAL

When you're trapped in addiction, you're not free at all. You're a slave to its power. In the back of your mind, you're always thinking...*when am I going to get my next drink, or hit, or candy bar?* Addiction is a prison and no matter what you do, you can't seem to break free. Denial is largely to blame for this and unfortunately denial is a major part of the addiction process.

When you're in denial you continue to use the addictive substance or engage in the addictive behavior even though you experience extremely negative consequences. You're unable to believe *in the reality of the situation.* I was no different. I was in denial and told myself: *I did not get drunk and crash my car into a gas pump. I did not just do five lines of meth. I did not just eat a whole apple pie and then force myself to vomit.*

I was unable to come out of denial because that would have meant I had to face my addictions head-on. I would have needed to confront my issues as an addict, and that overwhelmed me. As a result, I totally denied everything.

Hitting Bottom

Many people believe it's easy to quit drinking, or to stop using drugs, or to resist gorging on food. It may sound simple, but these people don't understand we can't "just stop." There is no simple remedy for any addiction. If there was, addiction wouldn't be so rampant today. Unfortunately, abstinence often proves elusive until the addict hits some kind of bottom.

I began having problems with alcohol when I was fifteen. Friends met at the local swimming hole one Saturday night and there was plenty of alcohol to go around. I drank more than my fair share. A cute boy flirted with me as we sat by the bonfire, then someone yelled, "skinny dip!" We obliged and jumped in stark naked. I remember making out with the boy, then wrapping my legs around him before I blacked out. When I regained consciousness, I was in the back seat of a moving car surrounded by men I didn't recognize. We were driving down an unfamiliar dirt road. If I'd had my wits about me, I would have been scared. Before blacking out again, I heard the sirens.

The next thing I remember is sitting at a desk in the sheriff's office and spilling coffee all over the desktop and floor. I sobbed uncontrollably because the whole situation was completely out of character for me. I was a good student in school and was known to be kind and polite. I didn't even swear. I felt ashamed. The halo on my head tilted a bit.

The next incident happened in a park. Two guys walked up and began chatting. Despite the facts that one was carrying a 12-pack of beer and I was only 16, I allowed them to sit down and join me. We drank and talked for a while, and then I discovered they knew someone I knew from the small town where I grew up. Because of this—and the effects of the beer—I decided I could trust them. Big mistake. Huge.

They told me our mutual friend was having a party that evening, and convinced me to follow them to the house. After we arrived, they forced me into the bedroom and threatened that if I screamed, they would "give me something to *really* scream about." Both men raped me, but I didn't call the cops because I blamed myself for getting into that situation in the first place and I figured the cops would too. Being raped should have scared me into not drinking, but it didn't.

The following year, I learned my boyfriend was cheating on me and had been for months, so I decided to drown my sorrows in a bottle of vodka. I hopped into my car and blacked out. The next thing I remember is flashing lights in my rear view mirror as I sped down the street. The cop ordered me to step out of the car and recite the alphabet. I began to sing, "ABCDEFG – HIJKLMNOP – HIJKLMNOP." I failed the sobriety test and began sobbing uncontrollably in the back of the police car. I was sent to juvenile hall and convicted of DUI. My halo had been revoked.

My college years and early twenties were spent drinking as much as I could while remaining a functional member of society. I was Polly Purewater when sober—but morally depraved when drinking. I tried to quit. Oh, how I tried! First, I tried restricting myself only to beer and then I tried only drinking on weekends. Both plans failed, so I tried limiting myself to one drink every half hour. That didn't work either and I repeatedly ended up drinking as much as I could…as fast as I could.

By my mid-twenties, my addiction had progressed. I visited a local casino on the Fourth of July to play keno and then watch the fireworks later that evening from the casino parking lot. I played a couple of games and then blacked out. I awakened in a totally white room and realized it was a hospital. There was a sheet over me, but I was half-naked underneath. I felt an uncomfortable sensation between my legs which turned out to be a clear tube containing yellow liquid. I could see it sticking out from under the sheet.

When the nurse came in, I asked, "What on earth is this tube?"

"That's part of your catheter," she said. I didn't ask what happened; I guess I didn't want to know. My head was pounding and I felt nauseated. I could remember drinking and playing keno, but nothing else. "Your blood alcohol level was about .40," the nurse said. "You should've been dead."

I vowed to quit drinking that day.

Several days later I attended a computer class for my job. Before class I stopped at a grocery store and bought a bottle of vodka. I added some vodka to a can of soda and drank it on the spot. Then I chugged the remaining vodka straight from the bottle, went to class, and blacked out. Again, I awoke in a hospital with a blood alcohol level of .40. I could have died that day—not only from the alcohol in my system, but also from driving into a gas pump when I passed out. I loved that '72 Chevy Impala convertible, but now the fender and hood were crunched.

I quit drinking for a few days, but addiction had its claws in me and it wasn't quite ready to let go. I continued drinking as much as I could, as often as I could. I was in deep despair. I had given up. I stopped questioning why I couldn't control myself; it didn't seem to matter anymore. Nothing did. The greater my desire to quit, the more difficult it became.

I was at the end of my rope...and there was nothing I could do about it. I believed alcohol would eventually kill me; I just hoped it would happen quickly. My days were a blur. I went through the motions, but coherent thoughts were few and far between.

One day on my way to work I stopped at a gas station and bought a bottle of vodka, then stopped at McDonald's for breakfast burritos and a large orange soda. I dumped out most of the soda and filled the cup with vodka. I drank what remained of the alcohol and then chased it with the spiked orange soda. I bought another bottle of vodka on my lunch hour and drank the whole thing before returning to my office. I blacked out.

The next thing I recall is lying on the floor at my house listening to the president of the company talking. He had apparently driven me home and was on the phone, telling my husband to come home and take care of his inebriated wife. *The president of the company I worked for—my boss's boss.* As he tried to leave, I grabbed his pant leg and told him everyone at work knew about the affair he was having with his secretary. Then I screamed, "You're not going anywhere! You're staying here with me!"

That was it! I had hit bottom! That moment marked the lowest point of my downward spiral. Horns now grew where my halo had been.

That very day, I entered rehab. The intake secretary had a tough time dealing with me because my thinking was still muddled by vodka. I told her I didn't want to lose my job and I meant it. I loved my work and it represented one of the few bright spots in my world.

She then said something that changed everything. She said if I didn't enter rehab, I was going to lose more than my job—I was going to lose my life. I knew this on some level, but hearing her say it so matter-of-factly jolted something deep inside my soul. The cold, stark reality of my out-of-control drinking hit me smack in the face.

Thankfully, not everyone needs some dreadful event to make them hit bottom. Some see their life heading in a direction they don't find pleasing and that's enough for them to overcome their addiction. Not me! I had to pass through the gates of hell many times. I didn't realize it then, but I had to experience every drunken tragic moment before I could hit bottom. This hell was necessary for me to triumph over addiction.

Running From Pain to Pleasure

After a few days in rehab, I felt hopeful for the first time in my life and the fire in my belly to stay sober was strong. Not all the patients felt the same way. Some found rehab horrible and wanted out as soon as possible. But for me, being in the hospital was like a cool drink on a hot summer day. I was ready for a change.

I was especially eager to attend regular group meetings. Listening to others tell their stories brought me many epiphanies and I enjoyed sharing my own story. One session covered the importance of reversing pleasure and pain. Being in denial about my addiction kept the good things about drinking at the forefront of my mind. In rehab, however, I could no longer deny all the bad things. Instead of running from the pain of low-self-esteem, feeling like an outcast, and paralyzing shyness (which alcohol temporarily cured), I began running toward the pleasure of self-healing and a sober life. Instead of running toward the temporary confidence alcohol provided me, I began running away from the painful consequences of consistently being drunk.

Breaking Down the Wall of Shame

My out-of-control drinking caused me to do horrifying things, which in turn caused me tremendous shame. Alcohol helped numb those feelings, but it also led me to even more shameful actions. It was a sequence I couldn't break. One factor perpetuating this cycle is the mistaken stereotype that all addicts are dirty, lying, waste heaps of human life with no willpower and no morals. Such stigmas only make it more difficult for addicts to admit their dependencies and increase the need for more substance abuse to numb the humiliation.

Group meetings helped me understand and put to an end to this cycle of shame. One group leader explained that addiction isn't the addict's fault. "Addicts don't choose to become addicted," he said, "they are merely left to deal with the consequences." He pointed out addiction is hereditary and may result in a "snowball effect" that gradually grows over generations. In my case, the snowball was gigantic by the time it reached me.

We also learned the body chemistries of addicts and non-addicts are actually different. People at greater risk for addiction have a different number of dopamine receptors in their brains and also different brain wave patterns. To my great relief, this proved addiction is not a moral issue. The hell I experienced wasn't my fault after all and even though I did some terrible things while drunk, in no way did that mean I was a bad person.

It was a comfort to hear others share their stories in group meetings. They all struggled with addiction and did repulsive things while under the influence. I thought I was unique, that I was the only one, but that was not true. Learning others went through the same agonies lifted a great weight from my shoulders.

Most of the counselors were recovering from addiction. This was undeniable proof that addicts could be intelligent, pleasant, upstanding citizens. This made it easier for me to admit my alcoholism and share my nightmarish stories. It was encouraging to learn our counselors had many years of sobriety under their belts and that they had changed their lives for the better. They were no longer controlled by alcohol or drugs; they were now in control of their own lives. They showed me sobriety is possible and that I could be happy leading a sober life. This may sound like an elementary concept, but until that point in my life, I was unable to grasp it.

One day in a group meeting I detailed many of the things I'd done under the influence, including daily drinking, one-night stands, and driving drunk. Jim, the group leader, looked at me and said, "April, I believe you're an alcoholic. Do you believe you're an alcoholic?"

"Yes," I said.

"Then your actions were right on track," he said. "What else would an alcoholic do other than drink and drive? What else would an alcoholic do other than go to work drunk and make a fool out of herself in front of co-workers? "You are right on track," he repeated slowly, "but now it's time for the next phase of your life where those things don't exist. You have the power to stop it— *right now.*"

This was a new way for me to look at life. I shouldn't feel shame for the things I did. I needed to admit my mistakes and take responsibility, but I didn't need to feel guilty about them. This was a breakthrough. Alcoholism is a disease just like epilepsy is a disease. If an epileptic's car hits a gas pump during a seizure, should they feel shame? Of course not. So why should I feel shame about doing the same thing? I needed to take responsibility for my actions, for sure, but then avoid making the same mistakes in the future.

I was still responsible for the things I'd done while drinking, of course, but I felt I had confessed my sins and was beginning anew with a clean slate. The overwhelming shame subsided and my wall of denial crumbled just enough to see daylight peeking through. Addiction is NOT a choice and it is NOT a moral issue. It is an equal opportunity affliction that doesn't discriminate. It affects young, old, tall, short, rich, poor, smart, stupid, good, and bad. Even though I did horrible things because of my alcoholism, I wasn't a bad person.

I straightened my newly discovered halo and walked away like a boss.

STEP ONE – SUMMARY AND WORKSHOP

Following each chapter is a workshop with items that contain activities with specific things you can do to help you stay clean and sober. I suggest purchasing a three-ring binder, a package of subject dividers, and a package of loose leaf paper to complete the written tasks. Alternatively, you can purchase a spiral notebook, or just use paper you have available. Transferring information from brain to paper reinforces the ideas and helps you remember the most important points. Items with an asterisk (*) should be written down.

- ✓ One reason for denial is to avoid confronting issues that cause you find to solace in your addictions. Another reason is the notion that overcoming your addictions may be too much to bear.

- ✓ Sometimes an addict must hit bottom before the reality of their addiction snaps them out of denial.

- ✓ Instead of using an addiction to run from pain, run toward the pleasure of self-healing and an addiction-free life. Instead of running towards the temporary pleasure of an addiction, run away from the painful consequences of your addiction.

- ✓ Addiction is NOT a choice and NOT a moral weakness. Nobody chooses to become an addict.

- ✓ There is no reason to feel shame for being an addict or for the things you've done under the influence. However, from this point forward, vow to stay clean and sober and never do those things again.

_____ * Make a list of negative consequences of using your drug of choice or engaging in your addictive behavior. Include any negative effects on your relationships, career, self-esteem, goals, or other parts of your life. The effects may also include things like hangovers, DUIs, job loss, divorce, embarrassment, financial cost, loss of friends, or anything else caused by your addiction.

_____ * Make a list of the positive aspects of staying away from your addictions. Include things such as clear thinking, peaceful life, dignity, happiness, higher productivity, better health, and so forth.

_____ * Make a list of things you did while under the influence of drugs or alcohol that caused you to feel shame. Ask yourself, "Isn't this what addicts do?" Are you right on track with the behaviors of a typical drug addict or alcoholic? You don't need to be ashamed of the things you've done. You are responsible for them—but stop feeling ashamed. From this point forward, vow to never again do those things. Now take this list and destroy it in any way you see fit, focusing on the fact that all these behaviors happened in the past and you have the power to stop them starting right now.

_____ * Begin a new list of things you've done that made you proud. If you can't think of any, make a list of things you could do in the future that will make you feel proud. Do something nice for someone else, tackle something on your to-do list, or accomplish something that makes you feel better about yourself.

_____ Go to your computer or your local library and do research on what causes a person to become an addict. Read about the science and the psychology of addiction. The more you learn about addiction, the more you'll,   realize addiction affects all kinds of people. You'll see that you're not an addict because you're a bad person. In fact, there could be many different reasons.

STEP TWO - PRACTICE ABSTINENCE

Make no mistake: abstinence is imperative to breaking the cycle of addiction. Tapering off or "slowing" your addictive behavior simply does not work. Having just one drink, doing just one line, or eating just one bite…is not an option.

If you go without the addictive substance for a certain amount of time, the cravings will diminish or disappear. Some people can quit on their own, but some don't quit until they're in a hospital or sent to prison. For others, a sudden decline in health or some other tragedy occurs that forces them to do something drastic.

Total abstinence needs to immediately follow the end of denial. Cravings need to be suppressed so one can keep their wits about them and take things further. It's nearly impossible to deal with the underlying causes of addiction while spending energy on feeding that addiction. The obsession of how and when to obtain the next fix will keep the mind too occupied to focus on recovery. Learn to recognize when you're feeding your addiction—and immediately stop doing so. Only then can you begin to recover.

Recognize Cross Addiction

When you stop using your drug of choice, there's a danger you may become cross-addicted to something else. Addicts commonly seek out replacement substances or behaviors. After I stopped drinking alcohol, I began a love affair with methamphetamines which helped deal with two serious problems I had—hunger and fatigue. I didn't have much money, but I always found enough for meth. I fell in love with this white crystal powder (and my house was spotless and my hunger disappeared!).

At first, I did just enough meth to maintain the high I sought, but eventually I found myself using far more. I cleverly emptied the drug into capsules and taped one capsule to each day on my calendar. That would allow me to limit my intake to one per day. It wasn't long, however, before I was ripping capsules off future days and taking multiple doses.

There were two other troublesome side effects to meth—huge patches of pimples on my face and paranoia. During the day I constantly looked over my shoulder, convinced I had a stalker. Each night, I pushed my dresser in front of my bedroom door so I would awaken if someone tried to enter my room. My addictive personality took over and I bought a "teener" (1.8 grams) every chance I got. Each day before work I did meth so I could function after being awake all night. At lunch, I took more to get me through the afternoon. Hour after hour, day after day, I kept this white magic on my mind. Finally, abstinence from meth was forced upon me when I lost my supplier. As much as I needed it, I didn't know anyone who supplied it.

Now that I was off both alcohol and drugs, another problem surfaced—my weight. Without meth, my weight varied rapidly both up and down. There's an old adage that says, "Losing weight is easy. I've done it a million times." That was me. I dieted and lost weight, only to regain it. I tried to control my food intake, but when I couldn't I forced myself to vomit. I was convinced that sugar, flour, and other processed foods made me happy. I believed a frosted brownie (or eight) would take my troubles away. Nothing could beat a candy bar to ease anxiety; it seemed chocolate calmed my nerves. Food was there for me when I felt lonely, depressed, or anxious. Unfortunately, binge eating also caused shame, guilt, low self-esteem, extra weight, and body image problems. Purging permitted me to believe I could overeat without gaining weight.

At the time, I worked in a real estate office where sinfully delicious desserts were delivered by title and mortgage companies. They were kept in a break room so everyone could share. One day I noticed a carrot cake with thick, cream cheese frosting, so I took a huge piece to my office. After wolfing it down, I sneaked back into the break room, took a full quarter of the cake, and hid it under napkins. I looked like a spy in enemy territory as I poked my head around the corner and looked both ways before entering the hall. I slipped into the women's bathroom and shoveled as much as I could into my mouth. If there was a heaven, this was it. My sweet tooth was getting the best of me.

When my bulimia became too much to bear, I considered my options. Stark, cold reality again hit me in the face. If I stopped throwing up after a binge, I would not only become obese—I might possibly develop diabetes or other health issues. If I continued my bulimic habits, I might develop decayed teeth, esophageal cancer, malnutrition, or even cardiac arrest. Even with these realizations, I couldn't stop bingeing and purging.

I tried every diet I ran across. I lost weight on the Atkins diet for a while, but then began eating the Atkins desserts. The sugar substitutes they contained caused me to have cravings and I would eat five or six at a time. I tried Weight Watchers, which helped for a few weeks, but after the novelty wore off, my cravings again took over. I tried Nutri-System, which cost hundreds of dollars each month because they shipped pre-packaged foods right to my home, but I ate all the chocolate desserts in one sitting.

One day I stopped at a local drugstore to buy three candy bars—one for right then, one for after dinner, and one for breakfast the next morning. I ate all three before leaving the parking lot.

I was so frustrated! Why couldn't I control my eating? Then a light bulb went on. It suddenly occurred to me that I was exhibiting the same out-of-control thoughts and behaviors with food that I'd had with alcohol and methamphetamines. I was obsessed with food. I couldn't stop thinking about when and where I would get my next food fix. This was a life-changing moment for me. I realized I was literally *addicted* to food. I searched the internet for anything I could find on food addiction and discovered many websites to choose from. I was surprised to learn there were even recovery programs for food addiction.

The program that worked best for me was Food Addicts Anonymous. It was the only plan to suggest abstinence from all sugar, flour, and processed foods—the substances most likely to cause cravings. Within a few days of implementing my new food plan, I experienced a miracle! My cravings disappeared! My belly growled from hunger, but I didn't feel the need to eat. I quickly dropped 30 pounds, but even more exciting was the fact I was now eating to live, not living to eat.

Before I was able to overcome my food addiction I needed to recognize it was, in fact, an addiction. I had to admit I was cross-addicted to processed foods, an admission made more difficult by the fact this subject is not widely covered in the media. As a result, many people don't realize processed foods are addictive substances.

People often comment on my willpower when they see me pass up bread at dinner or cake at parties. They do this because they don't understand processed food is an addicting. Passing up alcohol, drugs, or processed food is not a matter of willpower—it is a matter of eliminating them in order to quash the cravings and then working a recovery plan. This is the *only* way to take control…willpower is not enough.

How do you know if you have an addiction? When you consume a substance or engage in behavior that causes negative consequences—and repeated efforts to stop are fruitless. Addiction takes many forms. It could be shopping day after day until your credit cards are at their limit, or having sex with multiple partners. Perhaps, like me, you can't control how much you eat no matter how many diets you try. Regardless of the addiction, recovery requires an awareness of the addiction and a realization you can't merely decrease it slowly. The behavior must be completely stopped.

Boundaries and Discipline Versus Instant Gratification

An important element of abstinence is setting boundaries where none exist. Growing up, I never had curfews, chores, or restrictions of any kind. The freedom to do as we pleased was my mother's way of showing my brother and me how much she loved us. She did her best with what she knew, but boundaries are essential to a healthy childhood. They make children feel protected and teach important lessons about how to live life as an adult. Children need to feel part of something bigger than themselves, something to keep them safe and guide them through their seemingly massive reality.

Children develop a feeling of safety and confidence when they have rules and restrictions to adhere to. Otherwise, they are forced to rule their world by themselves—before they're ready—and they may tempt fate by exploring places that lie outside healthy childhood boundaries. Children without parental control are unlikely to set healthy boundaries for themselves later in life. I was out of control by the time I became a teenager because I had no boundaries growing up. I believed I could do whatever I wanted, whenever I wanted. Drink my liquid confidence (alcohol) for breakfast? Sure. Why not? Eat an entire chocolate cake for dessert? Absolutely! I desired instant gratification and I treated myself to it at every opportunity.

Unfortunately, this indulgent way of growing up made setting goals and working hard to achieve them impossible for me. I had no discipline. I didn't understand the meaning of sacrifice. I sought the easy solution and always took the easy way out. I avoided difficult decisions that may have favored a better life in the future, and instead worried only about what felt good at the time.

There are strong consequences that come with instant gratification and life without boundaries. If the addiction is sugar, the bathroom scales will reflect the indulgence. If the addiction is alcohol, the result may be blackouts, hangovers, and arrests. If the addiction is methamphetamines, pimples will sprout and paranoia will abound—not to mention the damage these addictions do to the body and the brain.

My brain was programmed to believe alcohol, meth, and processed foods were sources of happiness regardless of the negative consequences, and my inability to create boundaries made it difficult to resist the allure of instant gratification. Healthy boundaries and the discipline to adhere to them will not only help you stay clean and sober—they will improve your overall life. To remain clean and sober, the single most important boundary is *to abstain from the addictive substance or behavior.*

Attend to Self-Care

During recovery, self-care means taking care of the body's basic needs which, if not met, could lead to relapse. One powerful self-care tool is represented by the acronym HALT. Anytime you feel yourself becoming Hungry, Angry, Lonely, or Tired take a moment and fix the problem. Here's why HALT is so important:

Hunger and improper eating cause irritability, anxiety, and depression. Your best chance at recovery comes when you eat enough good food to help you function at your highest level. Your brain and your body both need proper nutrition to remain in tip-top shape.

Anger causes emotional turmoil in your personal or professional life, and it can negatively impact your overall quality of life. Work to resolve issues that cause you to feel angry. If you can't fix the problem, try expressing your anger in a constructive ways. Otherwise, you might find yourself engaging in your addiction to deal with your emotions.

Addicts have a tendency to isolate themselves, which may cause loneliness. *Loneliness* can also be caused by personal issues such as shame or low self-esteem. In turn, loneliness can lead to depression, a suppressed immune system, and even physical pain. If this is the case with you, work on finding underlying causes of loneliness and reach out to other people for help. It might be difficult for you, but you'll be surprised at how glad you'll be that you made the effort.

Finally, recovery requires energy. A complete change of lifestyle may seem overwhelming at times. Feeling *tired* may sound harmless, but fatigue can mentally and physically drain you to the point you're not able to fight for recovery. Protect your energy supply by making sure you get enough rest each day. Take a nap when you feel tired instead of reaching for another soda or cup of coffee.

Each of these four situations can pose a danger to your recovery, so take them seriously. They represent a risk of relapse because addicts are often out of touch with "normal" self-care. Learn how to handle each of these HALT feelings so addictive substances and behaviors aren't the remedy.

Throughout the day, take a moment to relax, close your eyes, and evaluate how you're feeling. Remain aware of your mental and physical well-being so you can control problems before they become too big to handle. Even if you can't solve a particular problem at that moment, simply being aware of it can cause it to lose power over you.

STEP TWO – SUMMARY AND WORKSHOP

- ✓ Abstinence is imperative to breaking the cycle of addiction.

- ✓ To suppress cravings, totally avoid your addiction. "Tapering off" or slowing down the use of a substance or behavior won't work.

- ✓ Abstinence needs to begin immediately after coming out of denial.

- ✓ Watch for signs of cross-addiction. Addicts commonly seek out replacement substances or behaviors.

- ✓ A lack of boundaries makes it difficult to resist instant gratification.

- ✓ Remember HALT. Avoid becoming Hungry, Angry, Lonely, or Tired.

_____ Immediately eliminate addictive substances, paraphernalia and other reminders of your addiction from your environment! It is vital to search your cabinets, drawers, purses, wallets and other hiding places. You can dump what you find down the drain, throw it away, or destroy it in any way you choose.

_____ Take a few moments to reflect about other addictions you may have. Addictions can take many forms including alcohol, drugs, shopping, exercise, and relationships. If you're consuming a substance or engaging in a conduct that causes negative consequences and repeated efforts to stop are fruitless, it may be an addiction. Look for episodes of bingeing or losing control. Telltale signs may also include declining health, secrecy, or the onset of negative circumstances. Do an honest evaluation about cross-addictions and then contemplate whether you need to take action or not. It might help to enlist the help of a friend or family member who may have a different perspective.

_____ Discipline is a necessary aspect of abstinence. To develop discipline, you must start small. Think of something you wish to accomplish but feel you don't have enough discipline. If you choose doing 50 pushups a day, start with five or ten and do them faithfully every day. Soon you can add more until you gradually build to your original goal of 50. Do you want to be disciplined enough to workout at the gym four times a week? Start small and go twice a week for a while. Or drive there four times a week but give yourself permission to back out after you arrive. Work your way up to a trip to the gym with a full workout.

_____ * Setting up and adhering to boundaries is a necessary part of abstinence. What boundaries will make your life better or make you feel better about yourself? Write them down and list intermediate steps you can take to achieve them. Perhaps you'd like to go to bed earlier each night. Set an initial schedule 15 minutes earlier than normal. Or, set a goal to watch only two hours of TV per night instead of three. Healthy boundaries and the discipline to adhere to them will create a huge difference in your life.

_____ Write HALT on several 3 x 5 index cards. Keep one in your car, one taped to your mirror, and one on your refrigerator. They will remind you at various points in the day not to become hungry, angry, lonely, or tired. Throughout the day, you should stop, close your eyes, and breathe deeply. Listen to your body and your mind. Evaluate whether any of these issues is present. Even if you can't fix the problem immediately, just being aware will put it in perspective and may keep it from overwhelming you.

_____ * *Hungry*. Make a list of nutritious snacks easy to grab as you run out of the house. A few of my favorites are fruit, celery with peanut butter and raisins ("ants on a log"), lunch meat and cheese, boiled eggs, caprese salad, and I often keep my favorite food handy—bacon! Always carry a snack in your car, your purse, or your pocket.

_____ * *Angry*. Write down ways to express and work through anger that don't involve addictive substances or behaviors. Burn up excess energy at the gym or through a different physical activity. You can scream into a pillow and punch it if that helps. Try breathing exercises and calming affirmations. You can try to take emotion out of the equation and think logically about a solution. While anger won't help a situation, rationally thinking about it might. Going for a walk is often helpful, as is clearing your head or talking things over with someone.

_____ * *Lonely*. Fortunately, there are a variety of remedies for loneliness. You can become a volunteer, rescue a pet from the shelter, or connect with people online who have interests similar to yours. The key is to keep busy with activities that bring you happiness. Make a list of things you can do when you feel loneliness setting in.

_____ *Tired*. Get plenty of rest. You deserve a restful, peaceful night's sleep every night. If you feel tired during the day, take a nap instead of reaching for the nearest caffeinated beverage.

STEP THREE - OUT WITH THE OLD, IN WITH THE NEW

Becoming clean and sober means you need to break ties with the past. Some of these connections will include friends or activities that helped perpetuate your addiction. If you don't replace old friends and activities with healthy substitutes, loneliness and boredom can set in which could make you vulnerable to relapse.

Find New Friends

The attack of New York's World Trade Center on 9/11 was a horrible tragedy. I can't imagine how anyone could murder so many people. What's the best way to deal with such an event?

Immediately after it happened, our country came together as never before. Why does it take a catastrophe for us to feel such a spirit of unity and oneness? We are all cut from the same cloth; we are all made of the same fairy dust. We are all on this planet to experience life together.

Unfortunately, some people feel they have no one to turn to. They haven't developed close bonds with others, or they feel a need to obtain comfort elsewhere. That's where drugs, alcohol, food, sex, or shopping enter the picture. An addiction can feel like a "friend" when you have no one else. Then, even if you seek out people for friendship, you gravitate toward people who share the same addictions.

During rehab for alcoholism, I met a heroin addict who was intelligent and easy to talk to. Soon he became my closest friend, but he was also poisonous to my recovery. After we developed a relationship, he moved in with me. A few months later, I discovered he was still using heroin. I didn't approve, but at that time being alone seemed worse than living with a heroin addict who was engaging in his addiction. Once again, I proved I needed to be put through the wringer again and again to learn my lesson. He lied to me, cheated on me, and stole from me for nearly two years. Finally, I kicked him out of my house.

Why did it take so long? I was still shy and unsure of myself, plus I lacked the support of good friends after I left rehab. I'd made no effort to stay in touch with anyone from the hospital and after only a few months, I stopped going to AA meetings. Had I gathered more friends to support my sobriety, they may have helped me make better decisions and put things into clearer perspective. Too many addicts in recovery maintain contact with those who supported their habit in the first place and shut out those who try to prevent it.

Recovery requires you to sever ties with anyone who enables your addiction. That is not an option. A support system of others with the same abstinence goals as you will help tremendously. They understand what you're going through and they may have been through similar situations themselves. Even befriending people who aren't addicts is very helpful when you need someone to turn to. Just having someone to root for you during recovery can build confidence and provide support when you need it the most.

Find friends who have positive outlooks and prefer to focus on the good things in life. Too many people, for whatever reason, focus on negativity. They thrive on pessimistic thoughts and toxic situations and you should stay away from them at all costs. Negative people are like vampires. They suck the positivity out of you and drain your energy. Avoid anyone who constantly complains.

Whatever your personality type, there are individuals who will appreciate you for who you are. You just need to find them. The internet makes it painless to connect with groups interested in the same topics and activities as you, and who won't try to change who you are. The key to success is to keep looking. There are plenty of people who will help and support you, so seek out like-minded individuals who can strengthen your resolve to stay clean and sober.

Find New Activities

Staying clean and sober requires that you abandon any old activities that may tempt you into using again. As an alcoholic, I would never consider a job as a bartender. Hanging out at a party spot where drugs and alcohol are common would not be a good idea either. Like me, you need to be sensible and stay away from temptation.

Free time can be especially dangerous when you're in recovery. After years of feeding your addiction, no matter what that addiction is, you may not have other hobbies. You may not even know yourself well enough to determine what activities you would enjoy. This is your opportunity to try new things, to find healthy activities to replace the unhealthy. Avoid anything that might involve addictive substances or behaviors. After I stopped drinking and using meth, I looked in the events section of the local paper and filled my calendar with things I thought might interest me. Some did, and some didn't, but I kept busy so I wasn't thinking about chugging vodka or doing lines of meth.

It's very important you get out and live life. The more experiences you have—good, bad, or indifferent—the more you'll be aware of yourself, other people, and the world around you.

Regular activities will help you feel comfortable in previously uncomfortable situations, which in turn will aid your recovery. At all costs, don't live like a hermit afraid someone isn't going to like you, or afraid you may encounter a problem. You might avoid a negative situation, but you need to experience uncomfortable thoughts and emotions in order to grow.

No longer can you use an addiction to numb your pain. If and when you experience negativity, your head will not explode (like I once thought!). Remember, when you open yourself up to new experiences you'll learn to more easily handle negative thoughts and feelings, and you'll allow your positive thoughts and feelings to shine through.

STEP THREE – SUMMARY AND WORKSHOP

✓ To find fulfillment, turn to healthy relationships and activities rather than addictive substances or behaviors.

✓ Seek out like-minded individuals who can help strengthen your resolve to stay clean and sober.

✓ Abandon old activities that may tempt you into using again.

✓ Free time can be dangerous to someone in recovery.

✓ Try new activities. Get out and enjoy life!

_____ * Make a list of people to call when you feel your resolve slipping. Keep the list in your wallet or purse and attach a copy to your refrigerator for times when you feel the call of addiction. Never hesitate to contact someone for help. Maybe it's a therapist or a hypnotist, but find people who are nonjudgmental yet strong enough to help you resist temptation. Do not give in to your addiction in a moment of weakness.

_____ * Make a list of places you can safely meet people. Consider this a "brainstorming" list and include everything that comes to mind. I met a lot of great people on meetup.com—a website offering groups for music lovers, line dancers, movie lovers, hikers, cheapskates, sushi lovers, political activists, and nearly everything else. You can also meet new people by volunteering at a local animal shelter, hospital, or food bank. Some colleges have classes for the local community, or visit a local church or spiritual center.

_____ * Make a list of activities you already enjoy and activities you would like to try. This is also a "brainstorming" list so include everything that comes to mind no matter how strange. You can go to a comedy club or rent a Redbox movie to watch. Perhaps you'd enjoy cooking classes, trips to the park, movies, painting classes, or concerts. Once you have your list, buy a calendar (or use the one on your phone) and fill the calendar with activities. When you're busy with things you enjoy, the deafening noise of addiction is more difficult to hear. Be sure to avoid anyplace likely to trigger your addiction.

_____ * Make a list of professional support programs in your area. You can ask your healthcare provider or search the internet for "recovery groups" or "spiritual support groups" or "addiction support groups." Your list can included AA and NA. Pick one that sounds promising and attend for a few weeks. Do you resonate with other people there? Does the program make sense to you? If it doesn't feel right, try a different one

.

PART I – CONCLUSION

Do I believe someone reading Part One of this book will immediately overcome their addiction? No. But I do believe that if you're at the end of your rope and you need a nudge in the right direction, this may be that nudge. There is no quick fix, no magic pill, and no one-size-fits-all cure for addiction. What encourages one person to refrain from an addiction may not deter the next.

It's not easy to discover what leads any one person to seek recovery, but this much is clear: for every addict and alcoholic, abstinence and a change of lifestyle are absolutely necessary. Even then, relapse can happen. Most important is to never give up. Once an addict hits bottom, overcomes denial, and works to achieve a clean and sober lifestyle, the beauty of self-healing can begin.

PART I – SUGGESTED READING

Addictive Thinking: Understanding Self-Deception by Abraham J. Twerski, M.D. (Center City, MN: Hazelden, 1990 and 1997).

The Addictive Personality: Understanding Compulsion in our Lives by Craig Nakken (New York: Harper & Row, Publishers, Inc., 1988).

Letting Go of Shame by Ronald and Patricia Potter-Effron (Center City, MN: Hazeldon, 1989).

Healing the Shame That Binds You by John Bradshaw (Deerfield Beach, FL: Health Communications, Inc., 2005).

Willpower's Not Enough by Arnold Washton, Ph.D. and Donna Boundy, MSM (New York: HarperCollins Publishers, 1989).

From the First Bite: A Complete Guide to Recovery from Food Addiction by Kay Sheppard (Deerfield Beach, FL: Health Communications, Inc., 2000).

The Wellness-Recovery Connection by John Newport, Ph.D. (Deerfield Beach, FL: Health Communications, Inc., 2004).

The Recovery Book by Al J. Mooney MD and Catherine Dold (New York: Workman Publishing Co., Inc. 2014).

Addiction and Recovery for Dummies by Brian F. Shaw, Paul Ritvo, and Jane Irvine (Hoboken, NJ: Wiley Publishing, Inc., 2005).

PART II
UNLOCK THE POWER OF
SELF-HEALING

Life support systems are amazing. They can keep a body alive even when it's barely breathing. But what about people with sound bodies who have become mentally, emotionally, and spiritually bankrupt?

People entering recovery frequently experience this situation. They're no longer ingesting their drug of choice or engaging in addictive behavior, but they still experience the same emotional issues that led them to seek solace in their addiction in the first place. Without intense effort, these addicts may relapse. Unfortunately, recovering addicts often lack the tools to accomplish such intense, internal work.

When I quit drinking alcohol, I failed to follow through and repair those aspects of myself that caused me to find comfort in drinking in the first place. I was still an unhappy, lost soul with no sense of self and no direction in life. Yes, I was proud I was abstaining from alcohol, but my inability to cope with life didn't immediately improve. While I didn't relapse to alcohol, I did become "cross-addicted" to methamphetamines and processed foods as a way to numb my pain and cope with internal issues. I still thought like a drunk and it took me years to gain enough confidence, self-awareness, and self-love to heal.

- ✓ Even after you abstain from your drug of choice, you can still experience the same emotional issues that helped perpetuate the addiction in the first place.

- ✓ Without intense effort to heal, addicts may relapse.

- ✓ Self-healing will allow us to gain confidence, awareness, self-love and the ability to handle life's problems which will help prevent relapse.

STEP FOUR - BECOME AUTHENTIC

Polly want a cracker? Parrots are amusing when they imitate words, but parrots don't understand what words really mean. They merely repeat things because it's their nature to do so, not because they know the English language.

Humans are often the same. We do things because we were trained to do so. We may mimic what our parents did or act according to what teachers or friends told us to do. We go through the motions because we think we're supposed to.

I have a close friend who attends church every Sunday. I once asked him about the philosophy of his church and why he believed in what his church taught. He couldn't answer. He didn't know why it was important to go to church or why he needed to repeat prayers a certain number of times. He didn't understand the sermons he heard each week. He went through the motions because he was trained to do so, not because he believed in the teachings.

The Chameleon

Life is not like a box of chocolates. The sweet, chocolaty goodness of even a "bad" chocolate doesn't begin to compare to the bumps and hurdles life throws our way. Some people thrive in tough times and come out smelling like a rose; others are especially sensitive and struggle to handle the inevitable rough patches.

I was the latter type. I was born with a birth defect which, after many surgeries, left a scar on my face. Early on, this didn't pose a particular problem. I was confident, athletic, and adventurous and I had many friends. Occasionally, kids would ask about the scar, but only because they wondered if it hurt. On my first day of seventh grade, however, I was picked on for the first time and it blindsided me. It hit me like a ton of bricks and their harsh words hurt me a great deal. I let them convince me that because I had a scar, I wasn't good enough. I betrayed myself and took on their beliefs as my own.

That began years of criticism for looking different. Kids I didn't even know acted like they hated me. They treated me as if I were defective and deserving of contempt. I had a few friends, but that didn't drown out the resounding stream of ridicule.

In youth, one's identity is formed in part by "mirroring" – a process in which your idea of who you are is mirrored back to you by the people around you. It shocked me when people treated me badly. Suddenly, I wasn't being treated like the happy, likeable, fun, sociable girl I thought I was and this caused tremendous turmoil at an impressionable age. This began my struggle with a growing identity crisis.

To cope with such negativity, I became numb—a robot with few emotions of any kind. I ceased to exist. I went through the motions of living, but somehow lost my authentic self. I was present on the outside, but inside was a dark, empty abyss. Anxiety and depression sometimes pierced the numbness, but my left brain took over and I became logical, rational, and analytical.

Many people battle abandonment issues, but abandoning yourself is especially devastating. This is what I experienced, and as a result, I completely shut down. I used numbness to cope with my uncomfortable thoughts and feelings. I lacked original thoughts and opinions, so I latched onto the opinions of others and weaved and bobbed like a leaf in the breeze. I became a prisoner, only doing and saying what I thought others wanted. I felt I didn't belong anywhere. As a result, I searched endlessly for an outside authority to validate me and make me feel safe. Not only did my thoughts and opinions come from other people, so did my self-worth and self-esteem. I was so desperate to be liked I continually sought approval from others. If someone liked me, then I must be worthy of being liked. But I had the demeanor of a beaten dog, so it was difficult for anyone to know me, let alone like me.

I attempted to be everything to everyone. I changed like a chameleon to others' idea of who I should be. The problem is everyone thinks differently. How could I possibly make everyone like me when everyone doesn't agree on what's likeable? My need to conform kept me hostage in a perpetual state of anxiety. When someone was rude, I wondered what I did to make them act that way then tried to change myself accordingly.

What I didn't realize at the time was changing yourself to make everyone like you only causes them to lose respect for you. It certainly doesn't make them like you. This was where alcohol came in. After drinking enough, I no longer felt paralyzed around others and I no longer felt the need to conform to their thoughts and beliefs.

Numbness was replaced by power and confidence. I said and did what was on my mind without fear of criticism. The chatty and outgoing person I became after drinking was not afraid of other people or fearful of genuine emotion. By drinking alcohol I avoided my "flawed" self and fled the fear of scrutiny from others. Alcohol became my escape from the miserable nightmare I'd created within myself.

You may have heard people say alcohol causes you to do things you want to do anyway but are too timid to do while sober. I strongly disagree. I was promiscuous when I drank. I risked my life (and the lives of others) by driving drunk. I was loud, obnoxious, and profane. In truth, I was a goody two-shoes hidden under an alcohol-fueled facade. Not only did my alcoholism cause many immediate problems, but I spent so many years drinking that my personality didn't develop naturally. The only time I revealed my personality was when I was under the influence and that was a false, distorted personality which only served to perpetuate my issues with my true identity. This identity crisis shut down my internal guidance system. I was so dependent on others for my values and opinions I no longer recognized my true feelings. It wasn't until my 30s that my eyes opened and I saw the truth of what was happening.

I was chatting with the cashier as she scanned and bagged my groceries. We were talking about something trivial – maybe the weather or the cost of groceries and I smiled and agreed with whatever she said. On the way to my car, I realized what I'd done and began pondering my odd behavior. Her opinions were different than mine, yet I had quickly agreed with everything she said. I wondered – Was *I afraid she wouldn't like me if I expressed an alternate view? Was I afraid of a confrontation? Where was my backbone?*

That meaningless conversation in the grocery store became an epiphany. In that moment, I realized I had a serious problem. For as long as I could remember, I focused on how I could get the most favorable reaction from others. I was so dependent on what others thought that I ignored my own feelings and thoughts. I agreed with everyone about everything and in the process betrayed myself. My fear of rejection prevented me from speaking my truth. I needed to be everything to everyone and this caused me to lose my authentic self.

Sometimes I walked around like a zombie and the rest of the time I spent as an actor. It has often been said you can't love another until you truly love yourself. I would expand on that by adding that you can't love yourself until you truly know yourself.

For too long, my true self had been buried under a sea of self-doubt, co-dependency, and a severe lack of authenticity.

I was a blank canvas on which I allowed others to paint my portrait. In order to paint my own picture, I had to look deeply inward. When a controversial situation arose, I noticed how I felt about it without taking into account other people's opinions. I paid close attention to my own thoughts and feelings to discover how I truly felt. Part of this process involves knowing it's okay to feel negative emotions. It's okay to feel sad or angry and to accept that all your feelings are valid. In fact, I discovered that certain negative emotions helped me pinpoint aspects of myself and my life that needed changing or adjusting. Mostly, I realized I shouldn't hide my emotions anymore. I needed to experience them to find out who I really was.

Give Up the Need to Conform

Some people like polka dots, some like stripes and others prefer no pattern at all. If we were all the same life would be quite boring, but because we're different we don't always get along. After years of self-reflection and self-healing, I realize that when I'm true to myself and what I believe, it doesn't really matter if someone doesn't like me. I know it's not because I'm *unlikable;* it's simply impossible for everyone to like everyone else. If I'm not popular with some people, it doesn't mean I'm defective or that I need to conform to their way of thinking. It simply means there are many unique personalities out there and I will click better with some than with others. When someone disagrees with me, that's okay. We can still respect each other for speaking our truths.

If you do the work necessary to discover your authentic self, you will feel greater confidence in your thoughts, words, actions, and emotions. This doesn't mean you shouldn't respect the viewpoints of others, of course, but it does mean you should be like a tree—you can sway a bit in response to other people and situations, but keep your roots firmly planted in the ground.

You can't please everyone all of the time, but you *can* please yourself one hundred percent of the time and be happier for it. When you quit seeking external sources for your identity and self-worth, you become your own master. When your thoughts and beliefs are your own, you will control your identity—and your destiny.

STEP FOUR – SUMMARY AND WORKSHOP

- ✓ We often do things because we were trained to do them, not because we believe in what we're doing.

- ✓ It's easy to lose your authentic self in the pursuit of the acceptance of others.

- ✓ It's impossible to make others like you since not everyone agrees on what is likeable.

- ✓ Make it a habit to look inward; pay attention to your inner thoughts and feelings.

- ✓ Each feeling you have is valid, regardless of what it is.

- ✓ Make a conscious effort not to adopt other people's beliefs.

- ✓ Do not be afraid to state your opinions.

- ✓ When you become authentic, you will demonstrate confidence in your thoughts, words, and actions. They will be your *own* truth, not someone else's.

- ✓ You can't please everyone all of the time, but you can please yourself one hundred percent of the time and be happier for it.

- ✓ When your thoughts and beliefs are your own, you control your identity and your destiny.

_____ Buy the book "Encyclopedia of Me" by Amy Krouse Rosenthal and each day complete one exercise. When you finish the book, you will have an encyclopedia about you! It makes self-discovery a fun process.

_____ * Write down anything you believe describes yourself. Include paragraphs on your appearance, your personality (funny, quiet, outgoing, impatient, adventurous, lazy), core values (such as honesty, devotion, truthfulness, fairness), key priorities, habits, particular strengths and weaknesses, plus anything else that describes who you are.

_____ Throughout the day, look inward and observe how you feel about certain people, places, and things. Paying attention to your thoughts and feelings will familiarize yourself with your true identity. If you're not certain how you feel, create a dialogue with yourself until you figure it out. Dig deep until your opinions come shining through.

_____ *Look Outward*. It's important to figure out who you are in relation to others. As you listen to people expressing their thoughts, analyze whether or not you agree with what they're saying. This may take effort and regular practice, especially if you're the type of person who typically agrees with anything others may say. In the beginning, you need to consciously avoid latching onto other's opinions and making them your own. Eventually, you will more effectively discern between your beliefs and the beliefs of others.

_____ *Social Media*. Some people believe social media is a waste of time and to some extent I agree. But interaction with others can be a useful way to learn more about yourself, and social media may be helpful in doing so. For instance, politics has fascinated me for a long time and my Facebook posts reflect this. I have Facebook friends whose beliefs are the opposite of mine and they regularly express their thoughts on my posts. Fortunately, we have lively, thought-provoking discussions without hitting below the belt or becoming angry. Also, these discussions provide an opportunity to examine my thoughts, see the other side of an issue, and change my opinion. Most of the time, they simply reinforce my opinions and strengthen my own beliefs.

Most people will respect your opinion, even if it differs from theirs. Remember the goal of discussing topics isn't to provoke an argument; it's to uncover your authentic beliefs. I use Facebook as my personal newspaper. I express who I am through memes, pictures, and posts. For someone who was previously an empty shell without authentic thoughts, social media is both valuable and therapeutic. It helped me learn about myself and my beliefs and it allowed me to be more comfortable stating personal opinions. So social media can be a good thing, as long as you're not substituting cyber relationships for real relationships.

_____ * Write your views on controversial subjects such as politics, gun control, capital punishment, religion, or other current events. Use your computer to research subjects so you can decide where you stand. Browse other subjects such as vacation destinations, music and games. What types of movies and television shows do you prefer? Forming opinions on various topics is one way to discover your authentic self.

_____ * List activities that might help express yourself. Be creative. Perhaps you'd enjoy painting, learning an instrument, writing in a journal, or planting a garden. Being creative and original can help uncover your authentic self. Select activities that fit your unique style.

_____ * Write down anything that helps express yourself. It doesn't matter what you write because what you feel may change from day to day. One day it might be a diary in which you record your thoughts. The next day you may choose to draw a picture and the day after that you may attach a newspaper clipping about something that interests you. Glue color swatches of your favorite colors, pictures, event tickets, or a list of goals you'd like to accomplish. This notebook will be an expression of you.

_____ * Search the internet for quizzes on self-discovery with titles like "Who Do You Think You Are," or "What's Your Personality Type?" Include your answers in your notebook. If you aren't on the internet, look inward and ask yourself questions that reveal who you are. Do I like this brown sofa? Did I act honestly in a previous situation? Why do I avoid certain people and gravitate toward others? Interviewing yourself is a simple and effective way to learn more about yourself.

STEP FIVE - VANQUISH VICTIMHOOD

The worst thing about being ridiculed by schoolmates was that I listened to them. I believed their message that I "wasn't good enough." As a result, my belief in myself went out the window and I became a recluse. For years, I avoided public attention and barely spoke. I lived in fear of being noticed, judged, or teased. I dreamed of working as a data entry clerk so my only relationship would be with a computer! I had allowed myself to become a victim of other people's thoughts and opinions of me.

People who feel victimized are prone to throwing pity parties for themselves. They complain to anyone who will listen about the rotten things that happen to them. I see it every day on social media. Sometimes, others jump on board and offer words of sympathy or support, but there's always another horrible day and another problem. Pity parties as far as the eye can see! Then people get tired of listening and support falls off. After a while, there's only one person left at the party—the pity-partier who is in a perpetual state of victimhood, feeling powerless and doomed for failure.

Sometimes, people who see themselves as victims believe revenge will ease their pain. They feel retaliation against the person who "wronged" them will make them feel better. They are mistaken. In truth, retaliation only invites ongoing conflict and unhappiness. Their desire to lead a happy, peaceful life becomes impossible.

Take Full Responsibility

Who is to blame for our addiction problems? Is it our parents' fault for not imposing boundaries or letting us know they love us? Is it our fault for not seeking better ways to cope with our pain? Is it nature's fault for causing us to be too sensitive or too weak to cope with hardship? Are schoolmates at fault for bullying us and causing us to feel inferior?

There is a problem with this question—it's no one's fault. Bad things happen to good people every day, including addiction. It's not the addict's fault. No one intentionally becomes addicted.

All the situations listed above contributed to my dependency on addictive substances. Yet I can't blame anyone else for my struggles. If I did, I would become a victim and that would mean other people have power over me. I've learned you can't change other people, but you can change yourself and your reactions to others. When you recognize your own role in your situation, it becomes much easier to change your life.

In addition to blaming others, we sometimes blame circumstances, however temporary, for our plight. "My car died and I couldn't get to work, so I was fired. It wasn't my fault; it was my car's fault." Only when you take personal responsibility for your actions can you gather together the power to change them. When you blame a broken-down car for being fired, you have no power to keep any job. If you examine the situation objectively, you may realize you were frequently late to work, or took extra-long lunches, or gossiped too long at the water cooler.

Ask yourself this: Had you been a great employee in the first place, would the boss have cut you some slack? Placing blame elsewhere is a popular way to avoid responsibility. But wouldn't your energy be better spent working to improve yourself? Accepting responsibility for your actions empowers you to change for the better. As a bonus, it allows you to accept credit when things go right.

Don't Take Things Personally

Why walk when you can ride? Sometimes we get sidetracked by minor bumps in the road. We trudge along, turning small obstacles into mountains that seem impossible to climb. No wonder it's frustrating to watch others glide along a smooth, flat surface with few apparent obstructions. Everything seems to come easily to them; nothing gets them down.

It's really about perception. When I was younger, I took everything personally. If someone was rude, I thought I deserved rude treatment. When kids picked on me, I thought my flaws warranted being picked on. I saw myself as a misfit. Everyone was against me and I felt very alone. But had I looked at things differently and not taken everything so personally, my early issues with self-esteem and anxiety would undoubtedly have been less severe and my quality of life would have been improved.

I have listed below a few typical problems. Each has two ways to respond—one that leads to misery, the other to a more peaceful, happy life. These examples may give you a good idea on how to improve situations in your own life.

PROBLEM 1

Kids can be cruel. If you look or act different in any way, kids will poke fun at you or worse. In my case, there was a girl in my class with a facial scar more noticeable than mine, so the other kids made fun of her.

Option A

When kids picked on her, she fought back. She didn't allow others to change her opinion about herself. She continued on with her life as usual, stopping only to wonder why bullies felt the need to make fun of her. She understood that it was the bullies with the problem, not her. She held her head high and didn't act like a victim. Since she didn't respond to insults, the teasing wasn't as bad as it might have been.

Option B

When kids made fun of me, I bought into it. I wondered what was so wrong with me that I was being treated this way. They affected me negatively, which was exactly the reaction they wanted me to have. I slouched when I walked and my self-esteem plummeted. I thought and acted like a victim which only made me an easier target. In a way, I created my own misery. I felt like a loser so others saw me as a loser. Not only did their verbal daggers penetrate my armor, I pushed them in further and twisted them which caused even greater damage.

Most likely, my attackers had things they would've liked to change about themselves, but I allowed them to convince me I was the only one with flaws. I allowed them to have power over me. They altered my perception of other people (people are cruel), and my perception of myself (I am worthless and ugly). Had I tweaked my perception a bit, I might have been able to think like the girl in Option A and blamed the bullies instead of myself.

After I quit drinking, I began to change my way of thinking. I assessed myself and the world around me more carefully. I realized that even with a facial scar, I'm beautiful. If others are rude or make fun of me, it's a reflection on them, not on me. Perhaps they're having a bad day or recently broke up with a boyfriend or girlfriend. Maybe they're naturally mean and unhappy so they pick on others to make them feel better about themselves.

PROBLEM 2

I recently met a man who asked me to his home for dinner and so I could help him write lyrics to two songs he recently composed. That same day, however, he accidentally sent an email meant for someone else. It said, "I just finished the lyrics for these two songs. Two songs in two days. Pretty good, right? The poet and English teacher will be here to edit/modify it tomorrow...lol." Since I am neither an English teacher nor a poet and he had already completed the lyrics, clearly he was making fun of me.

Option A

Had this happened a few years earlier, my happiness would have depended on him liking me. When he pleaded for forgiveness, I would have ignored his lack of respect and forgiven him. I would have obsessed on his betrayal and wallowed in my sorrow. I would have considered who I thought he wanted me to be and focused on trying to make him like me more.

Admittedly, I initially felt hurt and went into victim mode. I fired back a message asking if luring women to his home to write song lyrics that were already written was the only way he could get a date. I told him to enjoy eating his dinner alone. But then I analyzed why he treated me so rudely. I was sure I'd made a good impression; what was so wrong with me that caused him to act as he did? Then, I switched my perception.

Option B

There was nothing wrong with me! There was something wrong with him! A man who invites a woman to his house to write song lyrics that are already completed is a liar! Once I looked at the situation differently, I felt sorry for him and I focused on the self-respect I had for myself. Not only was I not a victim, but this experience helped me realize how far I'd come in my personal growth.

PROBLEM 3

When a friend searched his own name on the internet, some scathing remarks popped up regarding him, his business, and his social life. The remarks were posted on a website that encouraged people to vent their anger about others. While publicly posting negative comments about others is not considerate, he blew it way out of proportion.

Option A

My friend became obsessed with the anonymous comments and felt victimized by them. He called the number on the website and screamed threats and insults until he was blue in the face, but the following day the same comments were still there. Not only that, but the story was now the site's main headline. They'd retaliated against his verbal abuse by moving his story to the top of the page. When I pointed out you catch more flies with honey, he challenged me to call the website myself.

Option B

I did as he suggested and called the site to explain their story about my friend simply wasn't true. The man I spoke with was pleasant and suggested I email the editor with an explanation of why the story was unfair. He said if the editor agrees, the story will be redacted. I mentioned my friend's angry phone calls from the previous day and he said when they receive rude calls regarding a story, the site typically moves the story to the top of the page. Had the story been ignored, it would have moved to the bottom of the page as new posts came in. Eventually, it would have moved so far down the list it would have been lost in cyberspace.

My friend perceived evil all around him. He thought everyone was "out to get him." As a result he reacted like a victim which only made his problem worse.

Changing Perceptions

Sometimes it's difficult for us to change our perception. I once dated a verbally abusive man who often went into tirades telling me how flawed I was. He frequently told me I was doing, saying, or thinking the wrong thing. I tried to conform to his way of thinking and act accordingly so he would have a higher opinion of me, but nothing worked.

One incident woke me up to what I was doing. I had read a legal brief he'd prepared and emailed to me because he wanted my opinion. My computer was on the fritz, so I read his email on my phone. I was very impressed by his work and immediately called to tell him. When I mentioned I'd read it on my phone, he launched into a tirade about how inconsiderate I was to read his brilliant document on my phone. He'd spent ten hours writing it and said it was disrespectful to read it on a small phone. He said I should have found a computer to read it on and then called me "a small-town hick who doesn't know any better."

As he ranted, I considered his argument. Should I have found a computer? Would it have been worth the time? Even if I had, would I have understood the legal brief any better? No! He was being ridiculous! He hadn't just gotten up on the wrong side of the bed and he wasn't having a bad day. He was the type of person who consistently felt a need to belittle me and others. Instead of feeling like a victim, I looked deep inside myself. My actions had been logical and sane. I hadn't done anything wrong. I stopped feeling like a victim and instead felt sorry for him for being such a mean and miserable person.

The clouds parted, the sun came out, and I saw the light of day. I woke up to the reality of our relationship and lost all respect for him. The pedestal I had put him on disappeared. My confidence worked like an old balance scale—as I lost respect for him, I gained respect for myself. I concentrated on how wrong he was to berate me for minor things and I began to see myself not as a helpless victim, but rather as a powerful person unafraid to stand up for herself. Changing my perception was a major step forward in my self-healing.

I refuse to be a victim to anyone or anything, including the challenges of addiction. Every day I refrain from my addictions is another day I grow more powerful. Because I've overcome so much, I feel a type of strength and power that those with an easier life may not feel. I'm grateful for each and every day of my life—good or bad—because I choose to be. The old saying, "If it is to be, it is up to me" is very relevant when it comes to self-healing. Only by taking full responsibility and changing my perception was I able to take control of myself and escape the grip of a victim mentality.

STEP FIVE – SUMMARY AND WORKSHOP

✓ No pity parties, please!

✓ Revenge and anger only make you unhappy. Your goal is to lead a happy, peaceful life.

✓ Bad things happen to good people every day. It's no one's fault.

✓ When you blame others for what happens to you, you become a victim. Who or what you blame then has power over you.

✓ You must take responsibility for yourself and your life.

✓ When you accept full responsibility for your part in your addiction process, you gain the ability to free yourself from its grip.

✓ You can't change other people. You can only change yourself and your reaction to others.

✓ Shift your perceptions to prevent outside situations and people from affecting you.

✓ Each day you don't indulge your addictions you grow more powerful!

✓ Since you have already overcome great obstacles in life, you possess strength and power a "normal" person may not have.

_____ Think about a recent problem for which you blamed someone (or something) else. Search your mind and reflect on what part you played in the problem. Did something in your past contribute to the issue? Did someone hinder you? Was there an accident on the freeway that made you late for an appointment? If so, should you have left a few minutes earlier than you did? The more you take responsibility for your own life, the easier it is to change.

_____ * Have you been deeply hurt by someone and been unable to shed the negative feelings? Do you feel like a victim? Write that person a letter in your notebook. You don't have to send it, so let it all hang out! Call them any name you wish. Express all the emotion you feel about how they hurt you and why you feel as hurt as you do. Spend the time necessary to express all your feelings, then pretend they're in front of you and read it aloud. Scream and cry if it feels right. Read it again and again until you feel relief from fully expressing your emotions. Then, destroy the letter however you wish, and imagine all your negative thoughts and anger being destroyed with it.

_____ Has someone insulted you recently? Perhaps a friend or family member said or did something that hurt you. Imagine your negative feelings as a black ball of energy deep inside your chest and then ask yourself why you're carrying so much negative energy around with you. Imagine pushing it out into the universe where it will break into a million bits. Now, in its place, imagine a warm white light healing every part of your being. Repeat this exercise whenever you experience negative feelings from others. Over time, it will become easier and easier to replace negativity with warm, safe positive energy.

_____ * Write down why people say or do hurtful things. Your reasons may include breaking up with their boyfriend/girlfriend, waking up on the wrong side of the bed, or recently losing their job. Perhaps they were treated badly in the past, or they are currently under a lot of stress. Think of as many possible reasons as you can and remember there are no wrong answers. When someone said or did something that hurt you, one of these reasons may explain why. It may not have been anything you said or did. This doesn't excuse their behavior, of course, but it will remind you that they have the problem, not you. This helps shed the victim mentality.

STEP SIX - INDULGE IN SELF-LOVE AND SELF-ACCEPTANCE

Does a baby learn to cry? No, it's innate. If a baby is unhappy, he or she will cry. You too are born with instincts and ideas about yourself, including the inclination to love and accept yourself exactly as you are. Unfortunately, as you grow older, you learn not everyone thinks you're perfect. Most children get teased occasionally, but any child who is different in some way gets teased more harshly and frequently. If they happen to be especially sensitive, the teasing cuts more deeply than with those less sensitive. That's what happened to me and I needed a way to cope.

It was alcohol that swooped in to save the day! When I drank I didn't care what others thought. I spoke my mind without fear of judgment and I felt confident and beautiful. I felt normal—maybe even better than normal because my doubts and insecurities melted away. This was a beautiful thing *except for the fact my alcoholism nearly killed me several times*. I needed to find self-love and self-acceptance without my addictions.

Loving yourself allows you to trust your feelings and decisions. It helps you discover self-worth from within rather than seeking it from outside sources. It sets the standard for how others see and treat you. Some people go too far and love themselves to the point they become egotistical and arrogant. They believe others are beneath them, but that's not what I'm talking about. I'm referring to healthy self-love which allows you to treat yourself as well as you would treat anyone else.

Cease the Pursuit of Perfection

Orange bubble gum? Wait a minute! Bubble gum is supposed to be pink! Says who? When I was younger, I looked around and thought, "Everyone is so normal. Why can't I be normal?" They seemed happy, confident, and energetic. They talked and laughed together and I wanted to be just like them. But I was defective, an alien placed on this planet as a cruel joke. I desperately wanted to fit in, to be pink bubble gum like everyone else, but I couldn't shed my orange exterior. I was different.

Since I was teased so harshly, I tried to sidestep any judgment from others. I analyzed every thought I had which served as a thick filter between my brain and my mouth. As a result, it became difficult to express myself to others. I rarely spoke, even to my family. When others laughed, talked, or joked, I stared at them as if I couldn't understand what they were saying.

Learning to remain silent helped in some ways, but hurt in others. I drew less criticism, but my silence ostracized me even more from people around me. It contrasted with my natural desire to be talkative and outgoing. I wanted to be the life of the party, but I didn't permit myself to speak! Since no one wants to hang around a person who never speaks, I felt even more inadequate and flawed.

The teasing I endured also developed a deep need to appear physically perfect. My hair and makeup had to be just right or I wouldn't leave the house. I spent hours getting ready each morning. Not a hair out of place! Some people thought I wore too much makeup, but to me, makeup made my face appear more perfect. Since my facial scar was a common subject of comment, I caked on eye makeup which I hoped would divert attention to my eyes. My clothes were a different story. I was slightly chubby, so covering my ample derrière and self-proclaimed thunder thighs was a more difficult task. I couldn't wear clothes I deemed perfect, so dressing became another form of torture for me.

Even though I strived for perfection, I knew I was far from it. I harbored overwhelming anxiety about being judged, and my intense inferiority complex made me feel unworthy of friendship or admiration. When someone looked at me, I felt ashamed of my face and body. I felt ashamed to be me.

How I actually looked was unimportant because I convinced myself I was hideous. Until I learned to accept myself, I would feel inferior regardless of who I was or what I looked like. I held everyone in higher regard than myself. I was always at the bottom of the totem pole because everyone seemed smarter, prettier, happier, and more confident than me. Somehow, everyone seemed more *valuable* than me. Everyone else seemed right, and I seemed wrong—about everything.

I'm Perfect Just the Way I Am

I returned to college in my 30s and on my very first day I experienced my worst nightmare. We were told to prepare and deliver a ten minute speech the following week. My heart felt like it had been squeezed with a vice grip.

On the day of my presentation, I was afraid I would hurl my lunch right there in my car. Finally, I forced myself to walk from the parking lot to the classroom to find my classmates laughing and joking. They looked as if they didn't have a care in the world. I was overwhelmed with anxiety. I felt like my heart might beat itself out of my chest and I would keel over and die right there in the classroom. Then, something amazing happened.

As I watched others give their presentations, most showed signs of nervousness too. Some stumbled over words; a few spoke only briefly, not reaching the ten minute timeframe. As I watched, I had an epiphany. I had believed everyone else was confident and self-assured and that I was the fish out of water, but that night I started to realize I was actually normal. I was not an alien on this planet. I deserved space here like everyone else. My feelings that I was somehow less worthy than others began to fade, and it was a powerful revelation. At that moment, the Earth tilted a bit.

When my turn to speak finally arrived, I felt extremely nervous about walking to the front of the room. I still felt the slight need to vomit during my presentation, but I surprised myself by doing a good job. That speech represented the beginning of my extended journey toward self-acceptance and it helped nourish the idea that I'm just as valuable as anyone else. I began to notice instances of others feeling vulnerable and nervous. I didn't take pleasure in their obvious discomfort, but it reminded me they're on the same level as me. It strengthened my self-confidence and made me realize how similar we all are. Maybe, just maybe, I belong on the same pedestal as everyone else.

I could spend every minute of every day pursuing perfection and never reach it. The only option is to believe I'm perfect just the way I am and that my thoughts and feelings are as valid as any. I still want to strive to be a better version of myself, but I realize my goals will always be different than the goals of others. I will never be a six-foot, 125-pound model or movie star with full lips, but I'm okay with that. I'm perfect as I am and I love myself unconditionally.

You're Perfect Just the Way You Are

Nature is perfect. A flower doesn't need a facelift, nor does a tree need to lose weight. No two flowers or trees are the same, yet each is perfect. So why do people feel they need to change to be perfect?

Is there something about yourself you feel needs changing? Is it your height? Your weight? Maybe your quirky behavior or your weird sense of humor? Whatever the answer, you have two options. The first is to dislike the way you are and risk low self-esteem and unhappiness. The second is to embrace your unique qualities, whatever they are, and accept them as perfect just the way they are.

Everyone would like to change something about themselves. I promise you not one person is without imperfections, but there are no orange pieces of bubble gum. We're all from one big vat of pinkness and underneath our differences, we are all the same. We all pursue happiness and do the best we can. We all breathe the same air and have hopes, dreams, fears—and imperfections. We are all unique and wonderful beings. Perfection is a state of mind only attainable through the realization we're already perfect. It's what I am and what you are right now at this very moment.

Do Unto Yourself

You've often heard the saying, "Do unto others as you would have them do unto you." Sometimes that advice needs to be switched around. We need to remember to treat ourselves as well as we treat others. If you're an addict, that can be difficult.

There was a point in my life when I felt I was a failure. I criticized myself for mistakes, but forgave others for doing the same thing. I bent over backwards for others, but let them insult and disrespect me. I felt worthless, but I remained desperate for people to like me. As a result, I endured ridicule and contempt without fighting back. I wouldn't let a friend be insulted, so why would I allow it for myself?

This applies to you too. Treat yourself as you would your family or friends and *never* allow others to treat you poorly! You'll find when you treat yourself with respect it's easier to demand it from others.

Don't Compare Your Blooper Reel to Others' Highlight Reel

I know everything about myself. I've seen the good, the bad, and the ugly. Part of the reason I thought everyone was better than me is because I compared the worst of me to the best of others. It never occurred to me other people also get nervous, make mistakes, and have quirks. I didn't consider that others only put their best foot forward in public or that many wear elaborate masks to appear different than they are. I habitually compared my bloopers to everyone else's highlights. No wonder I felt inferior! Seeing the best in people is a good quality to have, but it's also important to see the best in yourself.

Nurture Yourself

You are the only *you* on the planet, so it's important to take care of yourself. Take time to learn what brings you happiness and peace and then do these things often. Don't feel guilty about treating yourself. When you take care of yourself, you're in a better position to help others. This is exactly why flight attendants instruct you to place the oxygen mask on yourself before helping others.

Nurturing yourself can take many forms, including major things like staying away from addictive substances and behaviors. But it can also mean small things like reading, taking a bath, meditating, or spending time with a supportive friend or family member.

Know You Are Worthy

Ever since I can remember, Mom had *just* enough money. We had a roof over our heads and food to eat, but little extra money. When she received her annual tax refund, something always seemed to come up that required the whole check. A needed home repair or new tires for the car took it all. She never seemed to feel worthy of more than just getting by. She expressed her low expectations to the universe, and the universe responded in kind.

Like my mother, low self-esteem made me feel unworthy. So after I quit drinking, I went to a counselor for help. When she asked why I believed I struggled with alcohol, I told her I thought I had low self-esteem. "Oh honey," she said, "everyone has issues with their self-esteem."

My first reaction to her statement was that she had no idea what she was talking about. To me, very few people had problems with self-esteem. In fact, everyone I knew seemed confident and sure of themselves. My next thought was that she would never be able to help me.

But it turned out she was onto something. Most people suffer a lack of confidence at times. Even egotistical narcissists need to boast about achievements to convince themselves and others they are worthy. There are many possible reasons you may feel unworthy and a good first step to changing yourself is to identify them. Did your parents make you feel this way? Maybe it was a boss or siblings or a significant other. Or perhaps every time you failed to live up to your own expectations, you felt a little less worthy.

Once again, you have two clear choices: You can carry on as you are and nurture feelings of unworthiness, or you can stop listening to negative thoughts which only undermine happiness. Inside each and every one of us is a magnificent soul worthy of the wonderful things life has to offer. Shed the inner critic that tries to convince you otherwise. Instead, connect to your perfect, whole self. Know you *are* worthy of good things in all areas of your life including love, peace, happiness, and security.

Don't Resist Compliments, Help, Love

If you don't love yourself, it's difficult to accept kindness or support from others. Growing up, when someone paid me a compliment on my hair, I would tell them I got lucky that day. If they complimented me on my intelligence, I said, "Sometimes my blonde brain actually works." *I couldn't accept a compliment.*

After moving to a new home, I decided to install shelves in my garage. I bought sturdy, heavy duty shelves that weighed a ton. Instead of asking for help, I spent much time and effort installing them myself. Had I sought help, it would have taken half the time and my neck and shoulders wouldn't have ached the next day; but *I didn't feel worthy of receiving help*, so I didn't ask.

I also didn't think I was worthy of love. If I had a boyfriend, I assumed he would date me until someone better came along. I was aware I gave a good first impression, but I assumed before long someone prettier or smarter would come along and steal him away. My lack of confidence and self-love repeatedly turned this fear into a self-fulfilling prophecy.

You betray yourself when you refuse compliments, help, or love. Instead, embrace each one and accept them with grace and dignity. It may seem awkward at first so you may need to practice; but don't be discouraged. Each time you accept a compliment or receive kindness and love, you reinforce the idea you are worthy. Simply say, "Thank you." Never be afraid to ask for help. Most people feel good about helping others, so in a way you're helping them too.

STEP SIX – SUMMARY AND WORKSHOP

- ✓ You were born thinking you were perfect, but you lose that perspective when you open yourself up to the opinions of others.

- ✓ No two trees or flowers look the same, yet each is perfect. You don't need to change to be perfect.

- ✓ The need to feel perfect can bring overwhelming anxiety, fear of being judged, or damaging feelings of inferiority.

- ✓ Strive to be a better version of yourself without pursuing perfection.

- ✓ You are perfect just as you are, even with your imperfections, so love yourself unconditionally.

- ✓ Do unto yourself as you would do unto others.

- ✓ You deserve to be treated as well as you expect your friends and family to be treated.

- ✓ When you respect yourself, you will receive respect from others.

- ✓ Treat yourself as if you are your own best friend.

- ✓ Don't compare your blooper reel to everyone else's highlight reel.

- ✓ When you take care of yourself, you're in a better position to help others.

✓ Accept compliments, help, and love whenever offered. Simply say, "Thank you" with grace and dignity. When you do, you reinforce the idea you are worthy of these things.

✓ Know you are worthy of good things in all areas of your life.

_____ * Write down ten reasons perfectionism causes problems. Here are some examples from my list: I compare myself to other people who seem more perfect than I am. If I don't perform perfectly, I feel like a failure. If I can't be perfect, I don't bother doing it at all. I'm often anxious because others may see my flaws. If you can't come up with ten, that's okay (we're not looking for perfection here), but write down as many as you can. It's important to appreciate how many negative feelings and thoughts are linked to striving for perfection. When you've finished, rip the list out of your notebook and destroy it however you choose. Write "I AM PERFECT JUST THE WAY I AM" in big letters on a new page. Because you are!

_____ * To rediscover your innate self-love, focus on good things about yourself. *What you focus on grows; what you ignore diminishes*. Write down ten wonderful aspects of yourself. For this exercise, you MUST come up with at least ten. Include anything from "I am kind" to "I say hello to the mailman every day." Write down anything positive you can think of.

_____ Look at yourself in a mirror and say "I love you and accept you as just the way you are. Do you feel resistance? Do you want to cry? Let it out. This is the healing process. The more reaction you have to this exercise, the more you need self-healing. The first time I did this, tears streamed down my face, and the more I looked at myself in the mirror, the harder I cried. After years of walling off my emotions, the floodgates opened. I was on my way to a love affair—with myself. There's something powerful about looking yourself in the eye and affirming the love you feel for yourself.

_____ * Think about how you would answer these three questions:

- What would I do tomorrow if I suddenly had the day free?
- What makes me feel energized and nurtured?
- What part of me needs attention to feel better mentally, spiritually, physically, and emotionally?

Make a list of ten ways to nurture yourself. Some ideas are taking a walk, enjoying a bubble bath, getting a massage, reading a book, watching a movie, cooking a favorite meal, meditating, getting a pedicure, or connecting with nature.

_____Pick a day on your calendar and label it, "My Day." Add your favorite nurturing items from the previous list and spend the day nurturing yourself. If you can't find a whole day to call your own, block out a few hours on a Sunday or choose a few items to do each day of the week and experience a little bit of nurturing on a daily basis. For example:

Monday: Spend an hour reading a good book.
Tuesday: Take a slow, relaxing walk around the neighborhood.
Wednesday: See a movie.
Thursday: Take a bubble bath with lit candles and scented bath salts.
Friday: Have lunch with a close friend or family member.

_____ Create your own space. This may be an extra room in the house or a corner of your bedroom. Decorate the space with favorite patterns and colors and display items you love. You now have a place you can escape to at the end of the day or when things become hectic. Use this personal area for self-nurturing. You can light a candle, meditate, read a book—or do anything else that causes you to enhance your feeling of well-being.

STEP SEVEN - ENGAGE IN HEALTHY RELATIONSHIPS

Here comes the bride! She looks so happy, as if her dreams have finally come true. Now she lives happily ever after, right? In a perfect world, we would all be happily married and living in bliss. But sometimes things go wrong.

Recognize Relationship Dependency

When you have little sense of self, no self-worth, and few boundaries, it's natural to seek validation from others. As addicts, we're especially susceptible to relationship dependency. We become quickly attached to a new relationship and its hopeful outcome so when the relationship falls apart, so do we. We excessively cater to the other person's needs and wants, abandoning ours in the process. The need to keep a relationship alive at all costs leads to neediness and clinging. These qualities usually cause the other person to push away, which only makes you more desperate to make it work. As an addict, I was too dependent on relationships. My need for a romantic partner was as strong as my need for air and water. If I wasn't in a relationship, the emptiness and depression were devastating. I felt unsafe and exposed. It was as if I was an astronaut in space, floating around looking for someone else's reality to grab onto. My reality had no boundaries and seemed strangely nonexistent. It was an empty abyss of nothingness which I navigated with fear, insecurity, and loneliness.

To ease these fears, I latched onto anyone willing to be in a relationship with me, which only triggered a downward spiral. Once again, my self-worth and identity were dependent on what someone else thought. My need to keep the relationship alive was so strong, I pandered to the person I was with and did whatever he asked.

My Heroin Addicted Boyfriend

Early in my recovery from alcohol, I met a recovering heroin addict. He had been kicked out of his house, so I let him move in with me. Things went south quickly. Often, I came home to find two used beach towels drying on the patio or two coffee cups sitting on the table. I suspected he was cheating on me, but he insisted no one else had been in my house.

One day I discovered common heroin paraphernalia—a needle, bent spoon with burn marks, and tiny balloons hidden in my closet. Of course he denied the items were his or that he was using again. Despite his obvious lying and cheating and the fact that I was supporting him, I remained desperate to stay in the relationship.

Why would I stay with a lying, cheating, heroin addict who took advantage of me? It made little sense, and it may be difficult to understand, but I was that dependent on the relationship. I was sleepwalking. He repeatedly pushed my limits. Because I had no boundaries on how people treated me, he got away with a lot.

Finally, I saw how foolish I was and kicked him out of my house. Instead of feeling crushing loneliness, I felt a surprising sense of relief. The sharp, crippling pain of being alone was better than being disgraced, humiliated, and repeatedly betrayed.

I now believe I met him for a reason. He helped me accomplish a profound and necessary change in the way I interacted with other people, and he altered the way I permitted others to treat me. Looking back, I'm grateful he disappeared for days on end and ignored my desperate calls to his pager. I'm grateful for his lies and the agony he put me through. As with alcohol, I needed to hit bottom with abusive relationships. Kicking him out became a defining moment in my life.

In the end, Mike make me realize even I had boundaries. Without him pushing me to my breaking point, I might have allowed others to treat me poorly all my life. Instead, I discovered I could control my own life by making important decisions and acting on them. This allowed my self-worth to peek out from the dark and be seen in the light of day. I was forced to a point where poor treatment was no longer an option. Once and for all, I realized I would rather be alone than with someone who disrespected me. I learned to remind myself that even though I loved him, I loved myself more.

The Art of Saying "No"

Do you strive to be a people pleaser? When others ask for a favor, do you say yes because you want them to like you? Do you say yes even though it means you will miss something important to you? If so, you need to understand this is a form of self-betrayal.

It's good to help others and lend a helping hand when you can. But if there's something more pressing you need to take care of or if you just don't want to do it, don't be timid about putting yourself first. You have every right to decline a request and not feel guilty. Don't over-extend yourself or do something you don't want to do in the hope the person asking will like you more because of it.

Sometimes it takes practice. It helps to memorize phrases that take the sting out of saying no. One of my favorites is, "I need to say no for now, but I'll let you know if something changes." When you respect yourself enough to say no, others will respect you as well.

The Benefits of True Friends

It's easy to feel the pull of isolation when you're experiencing the remorse and shame that comes with addiction. Loneliness and boredom are perilous, particularly for those accustomed to reaching for mood-altering substances or behavior. Friendships can help keep these emotions at bay and are uniquely soothing and healing to the soul, especially during recovery.

True friends will be there for you in time of need and they can help put things in perspective. They lift you up when you're feeling down and they won't criticize you for weaknesses. Friends provide feedback so you can monitor your behavior and feelings. They offer advice when you face challenges and help you adjust to the changes you're experiencing without engaging in your addictions. Friends ease your feelings of isolation.

Friends who are recovering addicts can be especially helpful by warning about potential difficulties and by reminding you there is happiness and hope in your future. Self-healing is aided tremendously with a support system of true friends.

STEP SEVEN – SUMMARY AND WORKSHOP

✓ Beware of relationship dependency.

✓ Do not abandon yourself to make others happy.

✓ Being alone is better than being disrespected in a relationship. You may love that person, but keep reminding yourself that you love yourself more.

✓ Stop being dependent on others for your identity and self-worth.

✓ What you *allow* is what will *continue.*

✓ Establish boundaries for how people can treat you.

✓ Saying "yes" when you want to say "no" is a form of self-betrayal.

✓ Don't be afraid to put yourself first. You have the right to say no and not feel guilty.

_____ Have you been in a relationship that created more misery than happiness? Did you stay, or are you staying, because it seems being with *anyone* is preferable to being alone? Do you need this person to validate your identity and self-worth? If so, this may be a form of dependency. Take an honest look at your relationships and identify your motives for staying in them. Understanding why you stay in a poor relationship may help you repair it or help free you from the chains of an addictive relationship.

_____ * Do you enter relationships without having boundaries? Do you allow yourself to be treated poorly or placed in unhealthy situations? Take a few moments to write down boundaries you think are acceptable in a relationship then evaluate whether your past and present relationships meet those standards. Boundaries may include paying back loans, treating each other with respect, having civil conversations about differences, how household duties should be split, or who pays the bills. It's healthy to set boundaries in your relationships.

_____ * Memorize phrases to take the sting out of "no".

- I can't give you an answer right now. Can you check back with me?
- I understand you need my help, but right now I can't.
- I'm honored you're asking, but I'm not able to say yes to that.
- I need to say no for now, but I'll let you know if things change.
- I appreciate you asking, but I can't do it.
- No, I can't do that. But here's what I can do…
- Under different circumstances, I'd love to. But my answer is no.
- I'm not ready to make that commitment right now, but thanks for asking.

Write your favorites in your notebook and commit them to memory.

PART II—CONCLUSION

After years of work on self-healing, I no longer depend on the approval of others. I don't change myself to make others like me and I have grown more confident and outgoing. My newly developed sense of self-love eases the fear of being judged. If I am judged negatively, I am at peace with that. Not everyone will think fondly of me, but as long as I love myself and do the best I can, the opinions of others have little importance.

My advice to you is this—do what you can to learn everything about yourself so you can come from a place of authenticity in everything you do. Search for the part you play in your life and take responsibility when you can. This will enable you to gain more power over how your life plays out. Love yourself as you are, including your idiosyncrasies and imperfections. You're not identical to anyone else, nor do you want to be. Learn to love your differences. Wear your scars like jewels and love the quirks that make you unique. Loving yourself is critical to healing and to feeling worthy of receiving love and acceptance from others. When you love yourself, you will find it easier to engage in healthy relationships because you will realize you deserve to be treated well.

PART II – SUGGESTED READING

The Encyclopedia of Me: My Life from A to Z by Amy Krouse Rosenthal (New York: Potter Style, 2014).

The Introverts Way: Living a Quiet Life in a Noisy World by Sophia Dembling (New York: Penguin Group, 2012).

What Type am I?: Discover Who You really Are by Renee Baron (New York: Penguin Group, 1998).

You Can Heal Your Life by Louise L. Hay (Carlsbad, CA: Hay House, Inc., 2002).

You Are More Than Enough: Every Woman's Guide to Purpose, Passion, and Power by Judi Moreo (Las Vegas, NV: Stephens Press, LLC, 2007).

Learning to Love Yourself by Sharon Wegscheider-Cruse (Deerfield Beach, FL: Health Communications, Inc., 2012).

The Ultimate Secrets to Self-Confidence by Dr. Robert Anthony (New York: Berkley Books, 2008).

The Courage to be Yourself: A Woman's Guide to Growing Beyond Emotional Dependence by Sue Patton Thoele (New York: MJF Books, 1991).

Codependent No More: How to Stop Controlling Others and Start Caring for Yourself by Melody Beattie (Center City, MN: Hazelden, 1992).

The Disease to Please: Curing the People Pleasing Syndrome by Harriet B. Braiker, PhD (New York: McGraw-Hill, 2001).

Addiction to Love: Overcoming Obsession and Dependency in Relationships by Susan Peabody (Berkeley, CA: Celestial Arts, 1994, 2005).

Breaking Free from Victimhood and Claiming Your Independence with Personal Responsibility by Joseph E. McGuire (CreateSpace Independent Publishing Platform, 2011).

Real Love and Freedom for the Soul: Eliminating the Chains of Victimhood by Greg Baer, M.D. (Rome, GA: Blue Ridge Press, 2007).

The Four Agreements by Don Miguel Ruis (San Rafael, CA: Amber-Allen Publishing, 1997).

Beyond Blame: Eliminating the Most Toxic Form of BS from your Life by Carl Alasko, Ph.D. (New York: Penguin Group, 2011).

The Everything Guide to Coping with Perfectionism: Overcome Toxic Perfectionism, Learn to Embrace Your Mistakes, and Discover the Potential for Positive Change by Ellen Bowers, PhD (Avon, MA: Adams Media, 2012).

Better Than Perfect: 7 Strategies to Crush Your Inner Critic and Create a Life You Love by Dr. Elizabeth Lombardo (Berkeley, CA: Seal press, 2014).

PART III
THE KEYS TO THE KINGDOM:
LIVE YOUR LIFE BY DESIGN,
NOT BY DEFAULT

Have you ever thought about changing your life, but decided the task was too monumental to take on at that moment? Sometimes you wait too long and instead of creating something good for yourself, you become angry at the universe for not doing more for you. This causes a general sense of depression and chronic bad mood which make drugs and alcohol seem like a great escape.

That's how I lived my life for many years. I floated along enduring whatever happened to me with no genuine inclination to change my life. I was more apt to drink a bottle of vodka, do a line of meth, or eat candy bars than create a better life for myself. Oh, the hours and days I wasted thinking about my next drink, or line, or cupcake! While I focused on my next fix, my sense of self remained deeply hidden. My thoughts, feelings, actions, and emotions were controlled by my external reality and my current drug of choice rather than coming from within myself. I felt powerless, as if I controlled nothing. I lived life by default.

Finally, after great effort, I managed to keep my addictions at bay. I quit alcohol, meth, and processed foods, but without my addictions, I felt lost. I was grateful to be free of my cravings, but I was unprepared to navigate my newfound freedom. I became restless and bored, sure signs I wasn't progressing toward my full potential. It took years to learn I could create a fulfilling life and become the person I wanted to be.

Do You Believe in Magic?

I believe certain principles of the universe are absolutely magical and the Law of Attraction is a perfect example. If you understand and leverage this powerful force properly, you can create the life of your dreams. According to the Law of Attraction, the universe will bring forth a reality that matches the vibrations you send out. Your thoughts, words, actions, and emotions vibrate at a certain frequency and can be used to create positive situations in your life. In other words, if you send out positive vibrations, you can create a positive reality.

Unfortunately, most of us live life by default. Sure, we wish for good things—but we don't purposely create them. Living life by default is part of the creation process—at least at a subconscious level—but it also creates uncertainty and anxiety. It inhibits our understanding of reality because we can't understand why our lives play out as they do. So instead of dealing with our lives as they are, we distract ourselves with our addictions. Using the Law of Attraction, you can distract yourself with the excitement of a whole new adventure—a life of your choosing.

You have the power to *create* your reality by deciding what that reality should look like. Then using your daily thoughts, words, actions, and emotions to raise your current vibration to the vibration you would have if you were living in that reality. Your subconscious will assume your goals are reality and make it easier for the universe to manifest them for you. You can use this principle to achieve your life goals and become your best self. When you think and act in a positive way, the universe will return that energy with positive experiences. Does this sound like the magic of creation? It is!

Thoughts, words, actions, and emotions vibrate at certain frequencies. The universe picks up on those frequencies and brings forth a reality that matches. To create a better version of yourself and the life you desire, be an observer of your thoughts, words, actions, and emotions. Align them to those you would have if you were already the person you want to be, living the life of your dreams. Remember, even when you're not intentionally creating yourself and your life, they are being created by default.

✓ If you understand and leverage the Law of Attraction properly, you can create the life of your dreams.

✓ The universe will bring you a reality that matches the vibrations you send out.

✓ Your thoughts, words, actions, and emotions can be used to create positive situations in your life.

✓ When you send out positive vibrations – you create a positive reality.

✓ Decide what you want your reality to look like.

✓ Align your thoughts, words, actions, and emotions with those you would have if you were already the person you wanted to be and living the life of your dreams.

STEP EIGHT - DESIGN YOUR KINGDOM

What time is it...*right now*?

The second that just passed will never come again. This is one of the tragedies of life. You believe you have all the time in the world, but today turns quickly into yesterday, yesterday becomes last week, and last week is suddenly last month. Before you know it, you are old and grey with little time to become the person you intended to become or to lead the life you wanted to lead. The years fly by whether you like it or not.

When you're unhappy with the present or have regrets about the past, you have two choices. You can wallow in sorrow and dwell on how things could have been different or you can decide today is the first day of the rest of your life. There remains much to achieve if you set goals and take the steps necessary to reach them.

Define Your Goals

The first step in creating the reality you desire is choosing exactly what you want that reality to look like. Imagine you're going to Hawaii for a week. Do you roam around aimlessly looking for something interesting to do? Or, do you plan your vacation and set goals to reach while you're there, ensuring you get the most you can out of your limited time in paradise? Life is the same way. We have a limited time on this planet and we should set goals to get the most out of our time here.

You can't get from "here" to "there" without a clear vision of where "there" is. You must have a realistic vision. If you're 5 feet 3 inches and want to join the NBA, you're setting yourself up for failure. But if you're 5 feet 3 inches and want to teach basketball to children, you've set a goal which is clearly realistic. It's important you take the time to consider what you would like to accomplish in life, both short and long term. What would you do with your life if you could choose? Where do you want to be in one, five, or ten years? Will you be in the same spot you are now, or will you be achieving what you want from life?

Also, if you set goals that center on material things such as buying a car, boat, or house, I suggest you take a second look at what's really important to you. Desiring material things is fine and there's nothing wrong with wanting a lucrative career or money in the bank, but don't assume you'll be a different person because you have money. The same fears and doubts will still haunt you. You may have more stuff and a bigger balance on your bank statement, but inside you'll be the same person.

A few of your goals should be associated with having a positive mindset. This is imperative when using the Law of Attraction to improve yourself and your life. You can't create positive things in your world if you're always wallowing in negativity or focusing on the worst part of every situation. A positive mindset makes it easier for the universe to help you create your best self and the life of your dreams, and you'll be happier along the way.

After you set goals, you may find that new ideas simply begin to appear. An idea may come from a song on the radio or a passage in a book. Don't ignore any idea that suddenly pops into your head because it could be the universe speaking to you, helping push you along your path.

Make Mountains into Molehills

Sometimes goals seem impossible to achieve. The mere thought of reaching them seems more a burden than a pathway to fulfilling dreams. There is a saying that helps solve this problem: "Life is hard by the yard, but a cinch by the inch."

Achieve your goals one small step at a time. If you do, they don't seem like impossible mountains to climb. Break large goals into smaller sub-goals and write down the smaller steps in chronological order. Each time you achieve a small part of your larger goal, you will experience a sense of achievement and motivation to tackle the next step. This applies to nearly anything you face, even house cleaning. When I look at my messy house on Sunday morning, I'd rather go back to bed than clean it. It seems overwhelming, but if I concentrate on one room at a time, it becomes doable. Before I know it, my house is spotless.

Writing this Book. When I began writing this book, I knew it would take a long time to finish because I didn't have the luxury of sitting in coffee shops and writing all day. Working in real estate to pay my bills and raising my children meant I had more important priorities. But I knew if I worked on it a little bit at a time, eventually my goal would be reached. I set a target of writing three times a week while drinking my morning coffee. I was only able to write a page or two each morning, but slowly my second book came together. The next challenge was organizing my notes into understandable book form. Again, I set a manageable goal of working two hours on each of my days off of real estate. Writing a book sounds like a huge undertaking—and it is—but breaking it up into bite-sized pieces made it achievable.

Going to College. At 36, I returned to college. Most of the credits from earlier years still counted toward my degree, but still I worried I was too old to be in school. It would take years for me to earn a degree. *Would it take too long? Was I really too old?*

I spoke with a counselor at the college about my concerns, but she pointed out the school recently graduated a 70-year-old. "It's not too late," she said, "but if you don't start now, it may never happen. Start now." I decided to do just that. When I looked at the classes I needed to graduate, however, I was overwhelmed. So, I decided to concentrate on a single semester at a time. That way it didn't seem like such a monumental task. Three years later, I graduated Summa Cum Laude with a Bachelor of Science degree in Applied Psychology. By the inch, it was a cinch.

Staying Clean and Sober. Early in life, my addictions ran rampant. I felt powerless over my life and my future, but alcohol made me feel invincible. It believed I could be whoever I wanted to be and live whatever life I wanted to live. I had liquid-induced confidence.

But over time, alcohol sent me on a downward spiral that threatened to ruin or end my life. A lifetime without drinking seemed impossible to me, but breaking it down into manageable goals made it feasible. As Alcoholics Anonymous teaches, take it one day at a time. Just for today, I will not drink alcohol. I can handle abstinence today—all day. Alcohol doesn't tempt me at this point in my sobriety and as long as I concentrate on staying sober *just for today*, it becomes do-able.

STEP EIGHT – SUMMARY AND WORKSHOP

- ✓ The first step in creating the life you desire is setting short and long-term goals.

- ✓ You can't get from "here" to "there" without a clear vision of where "there" is.

- ✓ Goals should align with what is most important to you.

- ✓ You must have a realistic vision of your goals.

- ✓ Money will not change the person you are. You will still have the same fears and doubts.

- ✓ Break each goal into small pieces. Life is hard by the yard, but a cinch by the inch.

- ✓ Each time you achieve a small part of your larger goal, you will experience a sense of achievement and motivation to tackle the next step.

Define Your Goals

_____ * Set your goals! You're going to set goals in three areas. The purpose of the first set of goals is to create a **positive mindset.** Negativity will thwart the most positive intentions, making this a critical step. The second set of goals will be to **create your best self,** and the third set will be to **create the life of your dreams**.
Be specific. Avoid sending vague or conflicting messages into the

universe. Forget what your friends or parents think. Make sure you set goals that make your soul happy. Make them so exciting you'll want to jump out of bed in the morning! Concentrate on activities that will fulfill you, make you happy, and create excitement in your life. What is your real purpose in life? What is your dream job? Where would you like to live? What type of friends would you like to develop? Would you prefer to be healthier? How do you want the world to perceive you? What are the natural abilities and talents you have that could help build a successful career? What would you like to learn?

Create a Positive Mindset

Close your eyes and imagine an alternate reality where you're happy all day, every day. Write down at least three goals for creating a positive mindset – For example:

- I am generally and happy person
- I am calm, cool, and collected.
- I have a positive outlook on life.
- I am optimistic.
- I see the positive aspects of every situation.
- I wake up every morning and smile.

Create Your Best Self

Close your eyes and imagine an alternate realty where you are your best self. Write down at least three goals you wish to achieve in order to become the best you can be – For example:

- I am healthy and fit.
- I speak well.
- I'm compassionate.
- I handle tough situations with grace and dignity.
- I dress well for every occasion.

- I exercise three times per week.
- I greet everyone I meet with a smile.

If you're having troubles with the list, select someone you greatly admire. Perhaps it's a friend, family member, or a celebrity with qualities you wish to emulate. Your goal isn't to be identical to someone else; it's to become a better version of yourself. Imagining good qualities in others often makes it easier to re-create them in yourself. Write these qualities down on the list.

Create the Life of Your Dreams

Close your eyes and imagine an alternate reality where you are living the life of your dreams. Write down at least three goals you wish to achieve in order for you to live the life of your dreams – For example:

- I live in a 2000+ square foot home.
- I drive a BMW.
- I have a bachelor's degree.
- I have close friends and see them often.
- I have a job I love that pays $70,000 per year.
- I am close with my immediate family and see them every week.

If you harbor doubts about achieving your goals, replace the voice in your head that says, "I can't" with a voice that says, "I can, watch me." Remember, you can't reach a goal you haven't set.

_____ * Write down each goal at the top of a separate page in your notebook and then write why each is important. It will help motivate you if you always keep in mind why your goals mean so much to you.

Make Mountains into Molehills

_____ * Under each goal, write down the sub-goals you'll need to achieve that goal. Is your goal to have a busier social life and make more friends? One of the sub-goals might include finding social groups based on your interests. Is your goal to lose ten pounds? Your sub-goals may include cutting out processed foods and joining a gym. List as many sub-goals as possible. They're your roadmap to success.

_____ * Write down a realistic start and end date for each sub-goal. Find a way to remind yourself to complete each step on or before the date you assigned it. You could also add each sub-goal to a calendar, a sticky note, or your phone calendar with automatic reminders.

_____ * Now that you've prioritized each sub-goal, write down a realistic completion date for the *overall* goal. Don't get discouraged or overly concerned. Perhaps your five-year goal will take seven years and that's okay! But, if you don't map it out and take action, it may never happen.

STEP NINE - USE THOUGHTS TO CREATE

Thoughts vibrate at certain frequencies. The universe picks up on those frequencies and brings forth a reality that matches. To create the reality you desire, be an observer of your thoughts. Then align your thoughts to those you would have if you were already living the life of your dreams and were the person you've always wanted to be. As often as possible, work on developing positive thoughts. Remember, even when you're not intentionally creating yourself and your life, your subconscious is creating them by default.

After buying a new car, do you begin to notice many more cars of that particular make and model on the road? That happens because your brain is focused on that specific make and model, so naturally you notice more of them. When I was pregnant I couldn't believe how many other pregnant women I saw. I thought a high percentage of women just happened to be pregnant at the same time I was! After my twins were born, I was surprised at how many babies I noticed. There was a baby epidemic!

What really happened is that my reality changed when my thoughts focused on being pregnant and having babies. *Anything you focus on grows.* When your thoughts send vibrations into the universe, the universe creates a reality to match those vibrations. Most people let their thoughts wander without guidance, so they live life by default rather than design. They still create their reality, but they do so subconsciously by merely reacting to situations. When you purposefully control what you think, you can manifest your own reality.

Focused Attention

The first step in using thoughts to create is to become a perceptive observer of your thoughts. When you notice negativity creeping in, make a conscious effort to push those thoughts away and focus your attention on something more positive. Think about a pet, your kids, a cloudless blue sky, or anything that brings a smile. Realize you have the ability to focus your attention on what brings you pain or on what brings you pleasure. There are an infinite number of thoughts you can choose from so choose positive ones that help create the reality you desire. The more positive your thoughts, the more positive the experiences you attract from the universe.

Each day focus on the good aspects of your world. Start in the morning and throughout the day make a conscious effort to stay focused only on positive things. It's okay to start small, because if negative thinking is part of your life, it will take time to change your habits. But if you tackle one negative thought at a time, a snowball effect will eventually make it easier to change your flow of thoughts to be more positive.

Are you depressed when certain memories flood your mind? Replace those memories with happier thoughts to create a different vibration. Are you anxious about something ahead in your future? Replace those thoughts with something positive that will happen. The effort to create positive thinking varies from situation to situation, but it is always possible. Choose thoughts that cause you to feel better and vibrate at a higher frequency.

You can also use *focused attention* to transform how you view other people. When you have negative thoughts about someone, begin focusing on what you like about that person. Your relationship can actually change because of it. This doesn't mean it's okay for someone to treat you poorly It means that when you're having issues with someone, you can use focused attention to make the relationship more bearable or even pleasant.

The Vouchers. I was staying at my timeshare when I received vouchers for dining in the adjacent hotel. The vouchers carried the name of the person who co-owned the timeshare with me. The first night of my stay, I used $75 in vouchers to eat at the hotel's steakhouse. The following morning, I again ate at the hotel, but in a different restaurant. When I handed the cashier my remaining vouchers, I assumed the restaurant would accept them. Surprisingly, the cashier refused to accept the vouchers and demanded I pay with cash or credit card. Ultimately, I paid with my credit card but left feeling very angry.

When I realized how angry I was about the cashier, I immediately replaced that thought with gratitude that I had been able to use vouchers the night before to enjoy filet mignon at the steakhouse. I couldn't change the situation, but I could change my thoughts. As a result, my mood became positive instead of negative.

Grandma. My grandma was physically and mentally abused by her husband for 30 years. Anyone near him had to walk on eggshells or feel his wrath. His negative energy was palpable. There was nothing she could do to change her husband into a kind and loving man, nor could she leave the situation. In those days, it was more difficult for a single woman with children to make it on her own. She was forced to remain and find a way to cope. She found that focusing on the love she felt for her two children made her life more bearable. Only her thoughts of maternal love allowed her to endure such anguish.

Bedtime Thoughts. I sometimes lie in bed for long periods of time with my eyes closed, trying to fall asleep, only to find I'm more awake than ever. That's my cue to mull over everything that has ever gone wrong or could possibly go wrong in my life! It's astounding how negative thoughts can swirl in my head before I even realize that's what happening.

What's the best way to avoid negative thinking while lying in bed at night? Before I get into bed, I make a conscious effort to review the good things that happened that day or earlier in my life. I persistently force negative thoughts from my head and replace them with positive ones. Not only do I fall asleep faster, it floods my subconscious with positivity as I sleep.

Visualization

Visualization is an extremely important tool in the creation process because it sends goal-oriented thought vibrations into the universe. When you visualize the goals you wish to achieve, it creates vibrations which help the universe bring your goals to fruition.

The Seminar. I once attended a seminar where a speaker demonstrated how powerful visualization is. He asked for volunteers, so I immediately raised my hand. He asked me to stand, hold my arms in front of me, and point my fingers straight out. He easily pushed my arms back down. He then asked me to visualize my arms filled with energy and directing a beam of light to an object across the room. He again pushed on my arms, but this time it required much greater effort. My focused thoughts created much greater strength in my arms.

Force Field. Several summers ago, I was driving down a freeway when I felt a bump and heard a loud thud. Another driver had merged into my lane without noticing I was there. Even though I was not at fault, I was forced to deal with the inconvenience of being in an accident. A month later, I was again involved in a no-fault accident. I was stopped at an exit ramp light when the driver behind me plowed into the back of my car. I immediately experienced negative thoughts. *"Seriously? Another accident? What was that guy thinking?"*

I decided to create something different. Now, every time I hop into my car, I take a few moments to imagine a white light force field surrounding my car making it impossible for other cars to penetrate my space. I ask others in my car to do the same so our energy is combined. Sometimes they give me an odd look, but I haven't been in an accident since.

I also use visualization to protect myself. I imagine an invisible shield around me which works like armor to keep negative energy out. Inside the shield, positive energy and my own strength blend in a magical whirlwind of protection which surrounds me.

Visualize to Create Yourself. Once you discover your authentic self—the one without addictive substances—you can use visualization to create an enhanced version of yourself. You can take the things you've learned about yourself and build on them, loving and accepting yourself just the way you are, but still striving to improve.

To use visualization to create your best self, imagine how your best self looks, thinks, dresses, acts, and interacts with others. What qualities do you admire in other people? Imagine yourself with those same qualities. Visualizing only takes moments a day, and it's a simple way to radiate a higher vibration and create a new reality by becoming your best self.

Meditation

There was an old lady who lived in a shoe. She had so many children…I bet she didn't have any time to herself. One important aspect of creation is taking time to be alone and quiet your mind. When it's difficult to find time in your day because of work, kids, spouse, or errands, it may seem as if you have little time to raise your vibration and create a positive reality. This is when you need meditation the most. Quieting your mind releases negative thoughts and helps you feel centered, relaxed and calm. It enables you to handle chaos more effectively.

Meditate to Create. Meditation aids creation by supporting visualization. You can create your best self and the life you desire by simply using visualization in your daily meditations. When I first learned this, I meditated while visualizing I was a successful author. I envisioned sitting at a book signing table and seeing people lined up out the door and around the corner waiting for me to autograph a copy of my book for them. I imagined the sounds they made, the smell of the bookstore, and the excitement I felt as I autographed each book. I imagined feeling happy and grateful as if my book was already helping a lot of people.

Each time I repeat this meditation, my vibration is elevated to a new level, the one it would be if the visualization were actually true. As a result, my vibration makes it easier for the universe to bring more good things to my life. I am attracting what I'm visualizing during the meditation.

Intuition. People base important decisions on what they *think* is best or on what others tell them is best. But in making decisions, it's important to tap into intuition. Remember, you're not a human being having a spiritual experience on this planet; you're a spiritual being having a human experience on this planet. Tapping into your intuition will raise you above the human experience and allow you to access information you need and want from your core level.

Meditation helps me tap into my intuition. It allows me to appreciate my true self, to know who I am in a way I had not previously experienced. It also makes decision-making easier. Knowing who I am at the core gives me the ability to make better decisions because I'm less fearful of them. When you quiet your mind, even temporarily, you will better understand how you truly feel emotionally, mentally, and physically. Conscious thought will not get in the way.

Anxiety. In one degree or another, anxiety has plagued me my entire life. Traffic lights even made me anxious. *What if the light turns red and I don't stop in time? What if I run the light and get a ticket?* Especially earlier in life, I felt anxious over small things which caused my heart to pound and my body to tense up. I found temporary, false relief in drinking alcohol, but there's a much better way.

Today, my anxiety is a minor problem thanks to meditation. Meditation quiets the noise of anxiety, boosts self-confidence, and reduces the stress of small aggravations that happen to everyone. With meditation, you will feel grounded as never before and more comfortable in your own skin causing reduced anxiety. Most important, reduced anxiety means less need for addictive substances and behaviors to calm the mind and distract you from daily problems.

Connect with your guides. Years ago, I was introduced to the idea of spirit guides (angels, helpers, light beings...whatever you would like to call them) from a friend with the ability to actually *see* them. From her I learned I have three spirit guides. One is a large, bearded mountain man named Russ. Another is a male named Milliken and the third is an Egyptian woman named *Saba*. The idea of having spirit guides was fascinating and I became determined to communicate with them.

I meditated and asked them to communicate with me. I received several images—a stick, the color green, and a cat—but clearly my imagination was merely producing random thoughts. The next time I spoke with my friend, I mentioned my experience and told her I was disappointed my guides didn't speak to me. She laughed and explained the images I had seen represented my spirit guides. Russ produced the image of a stick because he's a mountain man. As an Irishman, Milliken showed me the color green and Saba created the image of a cat because cats were sacred in ancient Egypt.

Heal your past. Life sometimes turns out different than planned. It's rarely a daily dose of sunshine and roses. Everyone experiences setbacks and endures bad days, but a single traumatizing event can change your life forever. It's tempting to use drugs or alcohol to numb the pain. Ironically, drugs or alcohol may have caused the traumatizing events in the first place. A better choice is to heal yourself from these events with meditation.

In college, my boyfriend visited his hometown during Christmas break. After he returned several weeks later, I watched him unpack. He pulled out a package of condoms and a stuffed bear with a heart sewn on it that read, "I love you." In horror, I asked, "Where did you get those?" He mumbled that his Mom had given them to him. Later, I learned the truth. He had reunited with an old girlfriend and they were now planning to live together. I had never experienced such excruciating pain. I would have preferred he beat me physically instead of breaking my heart because the physical pain would have been less severe than the emotional anguish I felt.

Decades later, this traumatizing event still impacted my relationships, so I decided to heal the scars. As I meditated, I visualized being back at the exact moment I learned of his cheating. I imagined walking up to my younger self ('80s garb, big hair, too much black eyeliner) and giving myself a big hug. I offered myself words of encouragement and told my younger self I didn't need him and that my life would be more fulfilling and happier without him. Tears poured out as I meditated. Even though I was emotionally drained, I felt deep relief which healed my soul. You will find this technique helpful for any trauma you've experienced in the past.

Initially, meditation was difficult for me. I am neither a peace/love nut nor a Kumbaya-singing, granola-loving person who found meditation natural or easy. In truth, I didn't care for it the first few times I tried it. It felt like wasting time when I could be doing dishes, writing, or accomplishing other necessary chores. Also, in the back of my mind, I believed I would have an immediate spiritual experience and instant knowledge of how to run my life. I was disappointed when this didn't happen since, as an addict, I want it all and I want it now! It was a lesson in patience I desperately needed. The results from meditation can take time, but it's well worth it.

STEP NINE – SUMMARY AND WORKSHOP

✓ Thoughts vibrate at a certain frequency and the universe will align your reality with the same frequency.

✓ Become and remain an observer of your thoughts. When your thoughts don't align with the vision of your best self or your dream life, change your thoughts.

✓ When you purposefully control your thoughts by focusing your attention on positive thoughts, you can manifest a positive reality.

✓ What you *think* helps determine your reality.

✓ To create a different vibration, replace bad memories with happy ones.

✓ *Thinking* positively will make you *feel* as happy as possible.

✓ Visualization is a powerful tool to send goal-oriented thought vibrations into the universe.

✓ Visualizing your goals will create a higher vibration and help the universe bring those goals to you.

✓ When life seems chaotic, that's when you need meditation the most.

✓ Quieting your mind through meditation releases negative thoughts and helps you feel centered, relaxed, and calm.

✓ When your mind is quiet, you naturally raise your vibration and manifest more positive experiences.

✓ When you meditate and envision your best self and your dream life, your vibration is increased to the level it would be if your visions were happening at that exact moment.

✓ Meditation quiets "noise" from the outside world and your mind, making it easier for you to tap into your intuition.

✓ Meditation helps your guides (angels, spirits, whatever you call them) communicate with you.

Focused Attention

_____ * Think of a problem that's troubling you at the moment. Is there a problem you fight on a continual basis? Try conducting a "negative purge" by writing about the problem in your notebook. Elaborate as much as you can by describing the problem and how it makes you feel. It may help to get the ideas out of your head and onto paper, and sometimes that can help you understand your feelings about the difficulty. After the thoughts begin to flow out of you, you may even find a solution.

When you've written all you can, imagine all of the negative thoughts and emotions being pulled out of you and being sucked into the words on the paper. The paper is like glue. Next, destroy the paper using whatever method has the most impact for you. Burn it, rip it to pieces, or throw it in the trash. As you're destroying the paper, imagine all of the negative thoughts and feelings being destroyed along with it. Next, imagine a positive wave moving through you as the negativity is being destroyed. This allows you to free your mind and focus on positive things that will bring you joy and happiness.

_____ * Pay attention to your thoughts. When you notice negative thoughts creeping in, write them down. They may include thoughts about you, other people around you, the world at large, pets, traffic, or anything else. Immediately think of a corresponding thought—a positive one—and write it down as well.

For example, if you have a lousy job, focus on the thought that you are employed. Search your mind for something positive you can take away from the experience and write it down in your notebook. Now, scratch out the negative thought so it can no longer be read, and repeat the positive thought as often as possible the rest of the day. Pay attention to your thoughts throughout the day and do this exercise. If you aren't able to write it down, you can mentally replace the negative thought with a positive thought.

_____ * You can do this with bad memories as well. If something happened in your past that plagues you with bad memories, replace bad memories with happier memories. Write down happy memories in your notebook. You can even put pictures in your notebook that remind you of happier times. Make a conscious effort to force the bad memories out with good memories and you will improve your mood.

_____ * Write down a negative situation you've experienced in your life. Then write three positive things that came out of that situation. You may need to dig deep. The good may not outweigh the bad, but there is nearly always some good that comes out of bad situations. The positive things could include that it made you stronger, it caused you to reevaluate your life, or it taught you compassion for others going through the same situation.

_____ Each day focus on the good aspects of your life. Start in the morning and throughout the day make a conscious effort to focus on only positive things in your world. It's okay to start small if negative thinking is a part of your life. It will take time to change your habits, but if you tackle one negative thought at a time, a snowball effect will eventually make it easier to change your flow of thoughts.

_____ * Think about having a million dollars in the bank (unless you already do, in which case imagine $50 million in your account!). The idea is to imagine a reality with more abundance. Write down how you would spend that much money. Would you buy a whole new wardrobe? How much would that cost? Subtract that much from your balance. Would you buy a new house? Subtract that too. Go ahead and list everything you would buy then take a few moments to visualize actually owning those things. The point of this exercise is to open your mind to receiving abundance from the universe, thereby making it easier to create a higher vibration and easier for the universe to manifest abundance for you.

Visualization/Meditation

_____ * A vision board is an excellent method to implementing the visualization process. It's a collage of pictures, words, and phrases showing things you'd like to have or accomplish. It could be a simple cork board or poster board from the dollar store, or a portion of your notebook. Regardless of what your vision board is made of, it will help you focus on the goals you wrote down earlier. Find pictures in magazines or newspapers that represent each goal and begin a collection. You may select a smiling face, a wedding cake, or someone enjoying a hike. Anything that represents one of your goals gets added to the board.

Put a picture of yourself in the middle of the board so your brain will equate you and the pictures you've chosen. Take another picture of yourself and cut out your face and glue it onto a picture of someone teaching, singing, or signing books in a bookstore or whatever your goals are.

Every day, look at your vision board and imagine having or doing those things. Sit in a quiet place and close your eyes. Reflect on one of the goals on your vision board and envision it fully. Use all your senses. Imagine the feel, sight, smell, taste, and sound of each one.

If you included a new car on your board, don't just look at the picture, imagine the view from the driver's seat. Picture the steering wheel, the dashboard, and everything else you would see if you were actually sitting in the driver's seat. Imagine how it sounds when you turn the key and start the engine. Does it roar when you press the accelerator or does it purr? Imagine the feel of running your hands over the seats. How does the steering wheel feel? How does the car smell? Then think how grateful you are for this beautiful piece of machinery and remind yourself you are worthy of it!

This is the process of creation. Your consciousness will believe it to be real and the universe will manifest it for you. It may take time to see results, but have faith. Just because you can't see the universe working for you doesn't mean it's not doing so.

_____ Imagine a force field around your body, protecting you from the negative energies of others. It may be a wall of white light or a glass barrier you can see through. Imagine the force field as a mirror deflecting the bad energy of others back into the universe where it can cause you no harm. The area inside the force field is full of your energy—positive energy—which is strong enough to protect you. You can also envision the energy of your angels or guides inside the force field helping you. You will find it easier to maintain a positive mindset when confronted by negative people and situations. You can also imagine a force field around your parents, children, home, or anything else you wish to keep safe.

_____ Associate a color with a specific goal. I had a college teacher who wore a green rubber band on his wrist. He explained to the class his family was poor, so he decided to create a new reality. Each time he saw the green rubber band, he visualized putting hundred dollar bills in his wallet. It worked so well he visualized putting thousand dollar bills in his wallet. He wore the green rubber band on one wrist and a watch with a green light on the other. When he checked the time, the green light reminded him to visualize putting money into his wallet.

You can use that method or be creative and take it even further. For example, you could put green sticky notes all over your house. Visualize putting money in your wallet or purse every time you see one. You could use pink notes to visualize being in love, yellow to represent happiness, or another color to signify a different goal. Each time you see that color, visualize achieving the goal it represents.

_____ Basic meditation. Find a quiet, comfortable place to sit or stretch out and take a few deep breaths. Relax each part of your body beginning with your toes, then your shins, calves, knees and so on. When I began meditating, I couldn't figure out why it was difficult for me to relax, then I realized my face was tense and my brow was furrowed. I tried to force my entire body to relax at once, but that was too much. When I relaxed one body part at a time, it became much easier. If you get bored or restless, count your breaths. Count each inhale and say "relax" on the exhale. *One...relax...two...relax...* Try meditating for five minutes at first and then work your way up to longer periods of time. Don't be discouraged if you don't have an out-of-body experience or an instant knowledge of how to run your life. Even if the benefits are subtle, they are well worth the time spent. Keep in mind that silence isn't empty; sometimes it's full of answers.

_____ * Meditate to achieve your goals. In your notebook, return to your list of goals and take a few moments to visualize an alternate reality in which all those goals have been achieved.

Consider one goal at a time and use your senses to visualize it fully. If one goal was to become a teacher, don't imagine seeing yourself teaching a class; visualize it from the teacher's perspective. Visualize the students looking at you from their desks. How does the classroom smell? How does the chalk sound as you write on the chalkboard? Visualize the sun shining through the classroom window. Then, when you are fully immersed in the scene, imagine how happy and grateful you feel you have the career you wanted.

Is your goal to earn a raise at work? Use your senses to imagine sitting in your office. How does it look, sound, smell and feel? Visualize your boss coming through the door with a smile on his face as he says, "I'm giving you a raise. You've worked hard and you deserve it." He sets a piece of paper on your desk. It's a paycheck with the exact amount of raise you desire. Then feel the elation and the gratitude in your heart! This is creation at its finest! Do this exercise for one minute. That may seem like a long time at first and it may initially be difficult to do, but with practice it will get easier. Increase the time you spend imagining each goal until you reach five minutes. The longer you focus attention on your scene, the quicker and easier it will manifest.

Each time you meditate using all of your senses, you raise your vibration, making it easier for the universe to create a reality to match it. Eventually you will be able to duplicate that vibration wherever and whenever you please—in your car, in line at the grocery store, or wherever else you happen to be.

Meditation is especially powerful if done before sleep. It allows your subconscious to marinate on your goals as you rest. Do this exercise every night to raise your vibration before falling asleep and your subconscious will help the universe make the visualized scene a reality.

_____ Fellow author Gregory A. Kompes (Kompes.com) created a meditation called *15 Minutes to Enlightenment* which can aid the creative process. This meditation includes three segments of five minutes each. For the first five minutes, clear your mind. When a thought appears, push it out in preparation for what comes next. For the next five minutes, think only about a single, important goal. You could use the scene you created in the previous exercise if you wish. Imagine your goal has already been achieved and visualize it from your point of view. Be sure to include all of your senses. Then, for the final five minutes, clear your mind again and push out any unwanted thoughts that appear.

_____ Meditation can help you connect with your guides, spirits, angels—whatever you call them. As you're meditating, ask questions you'd like them to answer and then quiet your brain. If a random thought intrudes, calmly push it out until you're only "listening" again. If your brain becomes too active, concentrate on your breathing. With practice, you'll learn to discern between answers to your questions and random brain chatter. In my early attempts, I received no information. Now I receive information more often. In fact, I used meditation to help write this book. Four or five days a week I lit a candle, quieted my brain, then meditated with pen and paper close by. When thoughts came to me, I immediately wrote them down.

_____ Many of us have a wounded inner child. Some say this is the part of us that holds many negative feelings from childhood such as loneliness, abandonment, hurt, fear, anger, sadness, or shame. After you start meditating, visualize your wounded inner child standing in front of you. Offer the child words of encouragement and love. How does that make you feel? The more uncomfortable you feel, the more you need this exercise. Give your inner child a hug and tell him or her everything will be okay. Feel the love in your heart pour out to the child, and then imagine yourself as the child receiving that love. Take your time and bask in the feeling of your inner child giving and receiving love.

_____ Meditate to heal the past. As you meditate, recall one negative event from earlier in your life. What happened? Where did it take place? Who was involved? Go back in time and imagine standing in front of yourself at that exact moment in time. Now imagine comforting yourself as the event is happening or directly afterwards. Give yourself a hug and tell yourself everything will be okay. Remind your younger self that many wonderful things are going to happen in life and that everything will turn out fine. What else might you say to yourself to alleviate the pain? Go back in time and turn it around. This time, imagine you are your younger self accepting the love and comfort from your future self. Enjoy the love and warmth you're receiving from your future self.

_____ Meditation can help you connect with your higher self. As you're meditating, ask your higher self questions. Then quiet your brain. If a random thought intrudes, calmly push it out until you're only "listening" again. If your brain becomes too active, concentrate on your breathing. With practice, you'll learn to discern between answers to your questions and random brain chatter. Getting in touch with your higher self is a powerful tool to creating your best self. Some may argue these two are the same.

STEP TEN - USE WORDS TO CREATE

Words vibrate at certain frequencies. The universe picks up on those frequencies and brings forth a reality that matches. To create the reality you desire, be an observer of your words. Then align your words to those you would use if you were already living the life of your dreams and were the person you've always wanted to be. As often as possible, use the most positive words you can. Remember, even when you're not intentionally creating yourself and your life, your subconscious is creating them by default.

Speak Positive Words

In order to raise your vibration, you must use positive words. Masaru Emotion, a Japanese scientist, conducted experiments on the effect words have on water. He labeled vials of water with words, some negative and some positive. After freezing the water, the vials labeled with positive words formed beautiful ice crystals. The water labeled with negative words formed misshapen crystals without much form or beauty. Our bodies are estimated at between 50% and 70% water. Therefore, it stands to reason that negative words cause us to vibrate at a lower frequency. This means it would be wise to stop complaining. When life looks dim or things don't go as planned, does complaining change the situation? No. It only wastes energy and makes you and the people around you miserable. Instead of complaining, use that energy to:

- Remove yourself from the situation
- Change the situation
- Change your perspective about the situation in order to accept the situation

This *doesn't* mean you can't talk about things you wish to change and how to change them. It also *doesn't* mean being fake or stuffing your feelings. It means cutting out the negative words and phrases that have no constructive qualities. There are ways to express unhappiness without complaining.

If someone asks you how your day was, but you've had a lousy day you can say, "I've had better" and leave it at that. If you must speak negatively, follow it up with positive words or a solution to the problem. For example, if you've just spent half an hour in line at the bank and you're describing the experience, you can say, "The line was a mile long, but I had a great conversation with the person in front of me" or "The line was a mile long, but it was relaxing to do nothing for half an hour while I waited" or "The line was a mile long, so from now on I'll go earlier in the day to avoid that problem." With this method, you're still expressing yourself by stating the problem, but you're switching the energy of the words by leaving the topic on a high note.

Self-Talk and Affirmations

It's time to talk about chatter—brain chatter. Addicts experience many regrets in life and these regrets can cause negative self-talk to become a habit. If you tell yourself often enough that you're stupid for making a mistake, your subconscious will soon believe that's true. Doing so on a consistent basis creates a low self-image and increases the chances you'll make similar mistakes in the future. *You cannot become a self-confident person while constantly criticizing yourself.* Positive self-talk can help you gain self-worth and self-love. It will raise your vibration and make it easier for the universe to create a more positive reality for you.

When you realize your self-talk is negative, switch the dialogue to something positive. If you say to yourself, "I am so stupid. Nobody likes me," immediately say, "Stop!" Then switch the message to something positive such as, "I am a good person and I'm doing the best I can. My friends and family care about me and love me."

Affirmations are a form of self-talk you can use to your advantage. They are intentional statements you repeat to create a specific effect. You can help create a positive mindset, create your best self, and create the life of your dreams by using affirmations. Choose affirmations that resonate with you. Some affirmations *feel* better and sound more appropriate. The wording of an affirmation is important. Keep them short and avoid referring to what you *don't* want. State what you *do* want.

For instance, if you want to reduce stress, don't say, "I am *not* stressed." Your subconscious will focus on the word "stressed." Instead, use positive words. Say, "I am calm, cool, collected, and centered." Also, use present tense. Affirmations such as, "I will own a Corvette" only tell your subconscious and the universe you do not own a Corvette. The affirmation should be, "I own a Corvette."

Never use "I want" in an affirmation. Don't say, "I want a job as a nurse." This only tells the universe that you don't have what you want. The affirmation should be, "I am a nurse." This allows the universe to align your reality with that affirmation. If you keep focusing on the fact you *want* things to happen, you will create more "want," not more results.

To create your best self, use "I am" affirmations. When I created my affirmations, I envisioned my best self and came up with, "I am elegant. I am compassionate. I am honest. I am confident." I say them out loud every day. The more I tell myself these affirmations, the more I become my best self.

You can even create self-love by using affirmations. "I love myself" is extremely powerful and deserves to be at the top of your list. Use your imagination while saying this affirmation, especially if you don't feel you love yourself. Anyone can imagine what it's like to feel self-love for a few moments and the more you do it, the easier it gets.

Be careful your affirmations are not so grand your mind can't believe them. If you write an affirmation that doesn't seem possible, substitute it for one that sounds more plausible. For example, if you don't believe the affirmation "I am wealthy" is realistic, you can say, "Financial stability is coming to me now." Then imagine the universe is conspiring to make that happen.

When you focus on positive affirmations, your subconscious will listen and help the universe make them a reality. Trust the universe will manifest your desires for you. No doubts...no worry...no negativity!

You can recite your affirmations whenever your mind isn't occupied with other thoughts, including while driving your car, working out at the gym, and before falling asleep at night. Set aside five or ten minutes to work on your affirmations several times each week and pay careful attention to the meaning of the words. Don't just go through the motions, imagine what you would experience if the affirmation were already true.

STEP TEN – SUMMARY AND WORKSHOP

- ✓ Your words vibrate at a certain frequency and the universe will align your reality with that same frequency.

- ✓ In order to raise your vibration, you must use positive words.

- ✓ Become and remain an observer of your words. Align your words to those you would use if you had a positive mindset, were the best you could be, living the life of your dreams.

- ✓ Stop complaining. It accomplishes nothing other than to make you and the people around you miserable. Instead use that energy to leave the situation, change the situation, or change your perspective in order to accept the situation.

- ✓ Positive self-talk helps create a better life and a better you.

- ✓ You cannot become a confident person while constantly criticizing yourself.

- ✓ When your self-talk is negative, make a note to turn it around.

- ✓ Regularly practicing positive self-talk and positive affirmations make it easier for your mind to think positively.

- ✓ When creating affirmations, keep them short and positive. Don't use "I want" in an affirmation, it only creates more "want."

✓ "I am" affirmations are the most powerful.

✓ "I love myself" should be at the top of your list of affirmations. "I am safe" can help you when your anxiety level is high.

✓ Work on affirmations when your mind isn't occupied with other things.

✓ Set aside five to ten minutes several times each week to work on affirmations.

Speak Positive Words

_____ Stop complaining! Complaining means you're wallowing in negativity and it does absolutely nothing to fix the problem. It only succeeds in lowering your vibration and making you and the people around you miserable. You can't have a positive mindset if you are always complaining about something or someone. Instead, do one of the following:

- Remove yourself from the situation
- Change the situation
- Change your perspective in order to accept the situation

_____ Think of a negative situation you've experienced. How would you describe it? Try following it up with positive words or a solution to the problem. For example, if you've just spent half an hour in line at the bank and you're describing the experience, you can say, "The line was a mile long, but I had a great conversation with the person in front of me" or "The line was a mile long, but it was relaxing to do nothing for half an hour while I waited" or "The line was a mile long so, from now on, I'll go earlier in the day to avoid that problem."

_____ Take the challenge. In the book *A Complaint Free World: How to Stop Complaining and Start Enjoying the Life You Always Wanted,* Will Bowen suggests challenging yourself to stop complaining for 21 days. Part of the process is putting on a bracelet (he suggests a purple silicone bracelet which you can order from the website, but a rubber band will work). Then every time you catch yourself complaining, move the bracelet to the other wrist and start at Day 1. This is an excellent way to train yourself to stop complaining.

Self-Talk and Affirmations

_____ Words can affect your vibration whether they're said out loud or in your head. Pay attention to your self-talk. When you realize it's negative, switch the dialogue to something positive. If you say to yourself, "I am so stupid. Nobody likes me," immediately say, "Stop!" Then switch the message to something positive such as, "I am a good person and I'm doing the best I can. My friends and family care about me and love me." It will get easier over time for your mind to automatically think positively.

_____ Are you constantly putting yourself down? Do you only have negative feelings about yourself? Or, maybe you're numb and have *no* feelings towards yourself. No matter who you are— whether you're a hippie who sings Kumbaya or a big, burly man, this simple exercise is critical. Look at yourself in a mirror and say, "I love you. You are perfect just the way you are."

Do you feel resistance? Do you want to cry? Let it out…this is the healing process. The more reaction you have to this exercise, the more you need self-healing. The first time I did this, tears streamed down my face and the more I looked at myself in the mirror, the harder I cried. After years of walling off my emotions, the floodgates opened. I was on my way to a love affair—with myself. There's something powerful about looking yourself in the eye and affirming the love you feel for yourself that turbo boosts the healing process. You can't expect to be your best self if you don't accept and love yourself.

_____ * Look back at your list of goals and create affirmations for each one. You will end up with a list such as: *I am happy. I am confident. I am intelligent. I am well-spoken. I am lovable. I am capable. I have a great job. I have a busy social life.* Write these affirmations in your notebook. You may initially reject such positive thoughts, but eventually they will become second nature. When I feel negative thoughts coming, my brain almost automatically switches to "I am beautiful. I am elegant. I am confident. I am well-spoken." I've said these affirmations thousands of times.

When creating an affirmation, ask yourself three questions:

- Is it short?
- Is it positive?
- Is it worded in the present tense?

Don't create "want" or "need" affirmations. Never say, "I need a new job." Say, "I have a job I love that pays the bills" and then imagine how your life would be if that were true. Don't say, "I want a Corvette." Say, "I have a Corvette" and then imagine what it would feel like to be sitting in the driver's seat of your corvette revving the engine. Add your name to an affirmation if you're having trouble connecting with it or if you want to make it more effective.

As you recite your affirmations, visualize each one to be true, and strive to have pleasant feelings about each. If you say, "I am confident" but don't really feel that way, at least imagine what it feels like to be confident. Soon the feeling of being confident will be easier to imagine, and your self-confidence will increase.

_____* What's the biggest problem plaguing you right now? What affirmation do you need the most? If you're unhappy with your job, use the affirmation, "I have fun at my job and enjoy my co-workers." Do you suffer from low self-esteem? Use the affirmation, "I love myself unconditionally. I am perfect just the way I am."

A very powerful affirmation for feeling overwhelmed by the world is, "It's okay…I've got this." Because of my past, I suffered from a lack of confidence in difficult situations. This caused great anxiety, not necessarily from the situation itself, but from my fear of handling the situation poorly. I feared that deep, dark emotional depression or intense, agonizing shame would set in. When I said, "It's okay…I've got this" and I imagined feeling strong, I gave myself power over the situation. I created a strong sense of self-reliance which enabled me to fight off negative emotions caused by a lack of confidence. This helped with situations I couldn't change and helped me approach life more effectively because I was coming from a more powerful and confident place. Write these powerful affirmations in your notebook and refer back to them whenever you feel overwhelmed.

_____ Post your affirmations in a conspicuous place so you read them every day. Write them on 3 x 5 cards and tape them to your bathroom mirror, or write them directly on your mirror with an erasable marker. Each time you see the list, read it. One excellent affirmation for your mirror is, "I love myself and trust myself. I look forward to the challenges the day brings."

_____ Put your favorite affirmations in your phone using a calendar app. Set it to repeat every day, then set the maximum number of reminders. My affirmations flash on my phone five times per day! When you see the affirmation pop up on your phone, recite it ten times while imagining it to be true. This is a simple and pain-free way to remind yourself to recite affirmations.

_____ Put a copy of your affirmations on your nightstand and read them for five minutes before you go to bed.

_____ Use the timer on your cell phone or oven and write the same affirmation five minutes. Do this for a week, then repeat the exercise with a different affirmation.

_____ For this exercise you'll need a cell phone, a pair of ear buds (Bluetooth ear phones work well) and YouTube. Search for subliminal recordings on whatever subject you feel is best. Include the word "subliminal" in front of the subject. For example, search for "subliminal live life to the fullest" or "subliminal increase self-esteem." Bookmark the recordings you like and save them to your phone. I listen to favorite recordings when I'm cleaning the house, driving, or shopping. It's an easy way to instill affirmations into your subconscious. You can also record affirmations yourself and include music in the background. Somehow, music seems to help the brain "listen" more closely.

STEP ELEVEN - USE ACTIONS TO CREATE

Actions vibrate at certain frequencies. The universe picks up on those frequencies and brings forth a reality that matches. If your actions are consistent with the "old" you and your "old" life, you will put out the same "old" vibrations which the universe answers with the same people and situations. To create the life you want, be an observer of your actions. Then align your actions to the actions you would take if you were already living the life of your dreams and were the person you've always wanted to be. Remember, even when you're not intentionally creating your life, your subconscious is creating it by default.

An important aspect of the Law of Attraction is action. It would be wonderful to merely sit quietly and use your mind to create a new life, but unfortunately it doesn't work that way. You must take action to make the changes you desire. There are two components to initiating action:

* ❖ Doing what is necessary to make your goals a reality, and
* ❖ Acting as if you are *already* the person you want to be

Take Action to Achieve Your Goals

Each of your goals should have daily steps you must take to achieve the desired result. When you break your goals into bite-sized pieces, it's easier to believe they can become a reality. It also creates a road map to achievement.

If your goal is to make new friends, take physical steps to make that happen. Search online for groups of people who enjoy the same activities you do and then attend their events. Search for concerts you might enjoy and purchase tickets. Take your dog to the park and strike up conversations with other dog owners. If your goal is to lose weight, research eating options to help you achieve your goal, then go to the kitchen and throw out anything that won't help you attain your goal.

Regardless of your goal, the most important thing is to take action *now*. Don't wait to begin. Do something today—*anything*—to get started and I promise you'll be grateful in the future. You will not progress if you sit and wait for the perfect time, the perfect day, or the perfect conditions.

Act "As If..."

Act as if you are the person you wish to become and are living the life of your dreams. Why? So your subconscious will believe it and send out higher vibrations. This makes it easier for the universe to manifest it for you! When you act "as if" you're destroying the vibration of *wanting* and creating the vibration of *having*.

If you are passionate about your goals, you will find it easy to act as if they're already a reality. When I decided to become a successful author, I *acted* as if I already was one. On days off work, I dressed nicely and went to my second office, a coffee house or library. If someone asked about my occupation, I told them I was an author even though I supported myself as a real estate assistant. I attended writing seminars to meet other authors and joined Meetup groups that had writers as members. In other words, I surrounded myself with the same people and situations a bona fide author would.

Would a better version of you curse like a sailor or calmly manage the stresses of everyday life? Does your best self speed around in traffic as if in a race or calmly drive down the road in peace with the other drivers? No judgments here! I'm just trying to convey that you become your best self by imagining your best self and then choosing your actions accordingly. Not only will you feel like a better version of yourself, you will also inspire others to treat you as if you already are.

You've heard "The rich get richer and the poor get poorer." That may be true, partly because wealthy people act as if they're rich and poor people act as if they're poor. Visit an upscale mall and act as if you have all the money in the world (no need to purchase anything). Stop by a Mercedes dealership and test drive a new car. These actions will send vibrations into the universe that are consistent with someone who is wealthy, making it easier for the universe to create that reality for you.

Whether your life is going great or calamity is striking, each second is a new opportunity to create your reality. Work on your goals now and work on them every day by taking action. Your actions can transform humdrum vibrations into exciting vibrations of dreams to come. What actions can you take right now to change the vibrations you're sending to the universe?

STEP ELEVEN – SUMMARY AND WORKSHOP

✓ Actions vibrate at a certain frequency, and the universe will align your reality to that same frequency.

✓ Be an observer of your actions, big or small. Make sure all of your actions reflect your goals.

✓ Every second provides another opportunity to create your best self.

✓ Take action daily to achieve your goals.

✓ Any action you take to achieve your goals will change your vibration.

✓ Regardless of your goals, the most important thing is to take action *now*.

✓ You will not progress if you wait for the perfect time, the perfect day, or the perfect conditions.

✓ When you act as if your goals have already been achieved, your subconscious will assume they have. This causes a higher vibration and makes it easier for the universe to manifest them for you!

Take Action to Achieve Your Goals

_____ * You must take action to create a positive mindset. Surround yourself with positive people. It's difficult to be positive when you have friends or family who are constantly complaining or putting other people down. The solution is to get out and meet more people. Make a list of ways to safely do this. Consider this a "brainstorming" list and include everything that comes to mind. I met a lot of great people on meetup.com, a web site offering groups for music lovers, line dancers, movie lovers, hikers, cheapskates, sushi lovers, political activists, and nearly everything else. You can also meet new people by volunteering at a local animal shelter, hospital, or food bank. Some colleges have classes for the local community, or visit a local church or spiritual center to meet people with the same interests as you.

_____ Immerse yourself in positive messages. Find books with positive messages or positive affirmations. Watch happy movies that will make you laugh or just generally uplift your mood. Figure out what kind of humor you like best (slapstick, dry, highbrow, self-deprecating) and then search for comedians who are known for it. Write down songs that put you in a good mood and create a playlist with just those songs.

_____ Read *Who Moved My Cheese* by Spencer Johnson. You can also watch the 16-minute video on YouTube. This is a story of four little beings that lived in a maze. They ate cheese every day, but one day the cheese wasn't there. Two of the beings stayed in the same rut, expecting cheese to magically show up. They spent their energy complaining and whining when it didn't. They wallowed in their misfortune and felt angry. The other two beings immediately adapted to the change and spent their energy finding new stockpiles of cheese. This is an excellent demonstration of the benefits of adapting to change, accepting the current situation, and being proactive when things don't turn out the way you would have liked or expected.

_____ Reread the sub-goals required to achieve your goals. Are you working on your sub-goals every day? If your goal is to make new friends, take physical steps to make that happen. Search online for groups of people who enjoy the same activities you do and then attend their events. Search for concerts you might enjoy and purchase tickets. Take your dog to the park and strike up conversations with other dog owners. If your goal is to lose weight, research eating options to help you achieve your goal, then go to the kitchen and throw out anything that won't help you attain your goal. Do something today – anything – that will get you one step closer to achieving your goals.

_____ * From your list of goals, pick out the most important goal and circle it. On a new page write down at least one thing you will focus on that will get you one step closer to achieving that goal. Put this information on a sticky note or on the calendar in your phone to remind you to do it. Write it with a dry erase marker on your bathroom mirror so you see it each morning. There are many ways to remind yourself to take action daily to achieve your goals.

Act "As if..."

_____ Take out your checkbook and think about something you desire. Pick something from your vision board or your goal list that costs money. Is your goal a new car? Write an imaginary check to a dealership for the full amount of the car you want. Is your goal a new computer? Write an imaginary check to Dell or Apple. Perhaps your goal is to take your family to Hawaii for several weeks. Write the imaginary check to a travel agent. As you write your check, visualize what it's like to have enough money in your account to cover it. This raises your vibration, making it easier for the universe to make it a reality.

_____ Act as if you have a positive mindset. You've probably heard that the simple act of smiling makes you feel happy. You can't feel unhappy when you're smiling, right? Try skipping and smiling and see if you can't kick the blues away. Take this a step further and use your creativity to *imagine* you're happy. What does that feel like? When you can imagine happiness for a few seconds, extend that to a few minutes. The more you do this exercise, the quicker and easier you'll be able to turn happiness on like a switch.

_____ Act as if you are your best self. Every chance you get, imagine your best self. Throughout the day decide whether the actions you're taking align with that vision of yourself. If they don't, at least you're aware of what's happening and next time you can act differently. In addition to feeling like a higher version of yourself, this exercise will inspire others to treat you as if you already are.

_____ Act as if your goals are already a reality. Dress for the career you want, not the one you have. If you're seeking a love interest, make space in your closet and imagine his or her clothes are hanging there. Sleep on one side of the bed to make room for a significant other. Is your goal to lose weight? Buy a pair of jeans in a smaller size or window shop for smaller clothing if you prefer not to spend money. Fake it 'til you make it!

STEP TWELVE - USE EMOTIONS TO CREATE

Emotions vibrate at certain frequencies. When you experience negative emotions such as fear, anger, jealousy, hatred, etc., you broadcast negative vibrations which the universe picks up on and brings forth a reality that matches. To create the reality you desire, be an observer of your emotions. Then align your emotions to the emotions you would have if you were already living the life of your dreams and were the person you've always wanted to be. You must work on feeling the most positive emotions possible at any given moment. Remember, even when you're not intentionally creating yourself and your life, your subconscious is creating them by default.

You can't create a beautiful life if you're filled with negative emotions such as sorrow or anger on a regular basis. Don't focus on your problems. The penalty for doing so is a life filled with negativity. *My house is so old and small. I can't stand my job. I'm so sad all the time.* Since anything you focus on will only grow larger, focusing on unhappy things is a big mistake. It's true that what you resist persists.

Is it wrong to acknowledge negative things exist or happen? No! You can't just ignore them and hope they go away. But you don't need to dwell on those things. See them for what they are, but continue working toward creating good things in your life by focusing on positive things instead.

As you work to change yourself and your life for the better, remember negative feelings can creep in and sabotage your efforts. If you feel anxious or impatient about not achieving all you'd hoped, you could thwart the creative process. It's imperative to feel content and appreciate what you have in your life right now. Remain confident your dreams will come true and that you're ready, willing, and worthy to receive them. No more wallowing in negativity!

Happiness

Every action we take is aimed at achieving the ultimate goal of happiness. I'm writing this book because writing and helping people make me happy. I will take out the trash today because a house that smells good makes me happy. I brushed my teeth this morning because having fresh breath and no cavities makes me happy. You get the idea.

When I was younger, however, I couldn't find happiness in anything. I turned to drugs and alcohol to numb my feelings and obtain a false sense of joy. The first couple of drinks made me happy; I felt exhilaration and confidence; but after the slippery slope of addiction took over, I drank so much I became unhappy.

The natural malfunction of an addicted brain, combined with the euphoria of satisfying a craving, masked the destructive results of addiction. When misery replaces happiness in everyday life, it's simple for misery to flourish. When that happens, the addict identifies more with pain than with happiness. Have you ever known anyone who gave you the impression they couldn't be happy *unless they were unhappy*? Or someone who wasn't happy unless everyone else was miserable? That is no way to live. When we're happy, we send out positive vibrations that help the universe create a more positive reality.

Always look on the bright side. Sometimes the world seems to be crumbling around you and there's nothing you can do about it, or at least it seems that way. What you *can* do, however, is change your inner experience. Focus as much as possible on what makes you happy and you will slowly move beyond negativity to a happier state of mind.

If you desire more money, you may be tempted to focus on the fact you're broke. But this sends out vibrations that you're broke, which causes your lack of money to continue. Be positive when thinking about money or any other goal. Focus on how great it feels when you deposit a check or have a few dollars left after paying bills. You have a choice: wallow in negativity or work to find happiness. When you feel happy, you create for yourself more opportunities to be happy.

There's no need to be a Pollyanna or walk around with a smile on your face every hour of every day. You can't always change negative events, so ignoring them is not the answer. Don't try to cover up emotions no matter how negative they are. Instead, focus on the best aspect of the bad situation—the one that offers the most positive emotion possible. If you start there, you'll find it easier to experience more pleasant emotions during the bad times. Eventually, you'll automatically feel more positive regardless of what's happening around you.

This doesn't mean life will always be rosy. Bad things happen all the time and it's easy to focus primarily on the negative side of events, but instead of focusing on the roadblocks, make an effort to focus on the positive things. Instead of fretting about the horrible life you lead, concentrate on the wonderful things you already have and the accomplishments that lie ahead. Focus on the good you see in the world. *You have the ability to place your focus wherever you decide.*

Can you immediately change your mood from sad to happy and content? Perhaps not, but intentionally choosing to focus on things that make you happier will move you one step closer to nirvana. Work to discipline your mind and this transformation will become easier with each passing day.

Life is too short to be unhappy. Have you ever wondered what happens when someone dies? I've heard that molecules of energy never die, they just change form. If you believe in some form of afterlife, why take life so seriously? If you don't believe there's an afterlife…then why take life so seriously?

View life as a playground where you can use your physical body to experience positive, pleasing sensations. Use your mind to develop into the most advanced soul possible, one capable of genuine love and forgiveness. Life is too short to worry about every little problem that comes your way. Each minute you spend in sadness or anger represents one minute lost forever. On your deathbed, you don't want to wonder how much better your life would have been if you'd spent more time being happy and less being negative.

Don't Worry, Be Happy. Most of my worry and anxiety comes from events that never come to pass, or on situations that don't turn out as bad as I expected them to be. Years ago, I signed up for a class on prospecting for clients via the telephone. I was in sales at the time and this seemed the most effective tool for building my business. As the class drew near, I began to worry myself sick about making so many phone calls! How could I possibly call random people and ask for their business? They would definitely yell and cuss at me, and I would have a horrible day.

A few days before the event my anxiety reached new heights, so I decided to approach my problem differently. I was pregnant with twins at the time and knew if I was under stress it could affect my health and, in turn, affect them. I decided to let go of my fear and just do the best I could. It didn't matter if people were friendly or not because I could be happy regardless. That decision allowed me to relax prior to the event. More worry and anxiety wouldn't change the outcome anyway. Why make myself miserable?

You probably remember a time when you were overcome by anxiety over some future event. Perhaps you're afraid to speak in public and you were scheduled to stand at a podium and make a presentation. Your fear may have made you physically sick. The next time you face such worry, remember it does no good to worry about the future. It doesn't make the future better; it only robs happiness from the present.

Right now—*this second*—are you facing an immediate problem? If not, then stop worrying about it! If yes, then take immediate action to fix or accept it. There are no other alternatives. There are no situations that justify feeling negative emotions for an extended period of time. There are only situations that need to be accepted and resolved.

Cut Out the "If-only-isms." Wait a minute! Where are you running off to? Are you heading off on another "If-only-ism"? We all do it. We all say "if only ____ would happen (fill in the blank), then I'd be happy." Or, "if only I had ____ (fill in the blank), then I'd be happy."

Most people believe more money would make them happy, but if wealth made people happy, then why do so many rich people commit suicide? Money doesn't change who you are, it merely presents a different set of problems. Sure, money might make you happy for a short time, but very quickly you would realize you still have the same hopes, fears, insecurities, and dreams you did when you were poor. Happiness comes from what's inside, not from what's outside.

The king of "If-only-isms" was probably my brother. Years ago I heard him say, "If only I had a Mustang, I would be happy." Finally, he got his Mustang and it did make him happy—for a while. Then he said, "If only I had an Expedition, I'd be happy." But the Expedition didn't bring lasting happiness either. I also fell into that trap. I told myself, "If only I had that job, I'd be happy." "If only I had that car, I'd be happy." "If only I had $10,000, I'd be happy." My days were spent looking for an imagined future, one that would finally make me happy. I was never present in the moment or happy with what I had.

If you're like I was, you must change your ideas about what will make you happy. If you look for outside sources of happiness, you will be embarking on a frustrating, never-ending quest. You will never be happy. "If only I had this" or "If only that would happen" should never be followed by "then I'd be happy." You must strive to achieve your goals, but recognize that your happiness isn't contingent on them. Change "if only I had this or that" to "I am happy right now, in this moment." This will send out positive vibrations to the universe, making it easier for your goals to manifest.

Love vs. Fear. Many books, articles, and courses have been written about the love-versus-fear concept, and for good reason. Fear causes you to tense up and hold onto what you have as tightly as possible. Love causes the opposite reaction. It expands your world and allows you to accept what is. Unfortunately, fear often comes disguised as love.

For example, as an alcoholic, I "loved" alcohol—or so I thought. Actually, I lived in fear of people judging me and I needed alcohol to mask that fear. In relationships, I "loved" the person I was with so I held on as tightly as I could. It wasn't love at all causing me to hold on so tightly, it was fear. Since one of my greatest fears was being alone, I lived constantly in a "what if" state. _What if he stops loving me? What if he cheats on me?_ As a result, I was tense and anxious in every relationship. When I should have been basking in love, I was ruining the relationship with skepticism and suspicion.

This has nothing to do with the healthy type of fear that keeps you physically safe. I'm speaking about a deep, internal fear that plagues your mind and causes you to act and think negatively. It prevents you from leading a happy life. When you come from a place of love, you permit yourself to be happy and live life's purpose. When you love yourself, you create positive feelings that enable the universe to return more love and happiness. But when you fear aspects of yourself or the world around you, you relinquish the ability to attract a positive reality.

If you pay close attention to your emotions, you can immediately recognize whether they are positive or negative. If they are positive, they are most likely coming from a place of love. If they're negative, fear is often the culprit. Switching your reactions from "fear-based" to "love-based" will invariably produce a higher version of yourself.

Change the way you look at things. It's often easier to change your requirement for happiness than to change an unhappy situation. It might be difficult to transform your thinking, and it takes practice, but if you do you'll be able to let go and accept any situation for what it is. This means changing how you feel about things that make you unhappy instead of demanding life unfold in a certain way. Does your spouse really need to stop an annoying habit for you to find happiness? Does a co-worker have to stop slacking off? Do family members need to quit bickering for you to feel happy?

Here's the right question to ask yourself: should you give others the power to make you happy or unhappy? No! You can choose to be happy regardless of what's happening, especially if you're willing to make changes in your requirements for happiness.

I can't stress enough how important my next sentence is. *Your feelings about a person or situation are more important to your happiness than the person or situation itself.* What you desire from a person or situation shouldn't be a requirement for your happiness. It should be a *preference*. If you make it a requirement, you're giving the other person or situation power over your happiness.

Everything you need to create happiness lies within you. You are complete as you are. You are enough. Does this mean you shouldn't take actions to improve a bad situation? No! But you can be happier when you remember it's not the problem itself causing your unhappiness, it's your attitude about the problem. If you can grasp this concept, you can think more clearly and be more effective at changing the situation. And you'll be happier while doing it.

Negative Emotions. No one feels happy all the time. The most positive person you know sometimes feels down in the dumps. There are days, for no apparent reason, I am full of sorrow and nothing cheers me up. If I were to win the lottery, I would still be depressed. Other times I feel suddenly anxious, my heart pounds and I worry about the most trivial things. PMS may explain some of these "off" times, but my mild depression could also be triggered by drinking too much caffeine. Sometimes, for no reason at all, one little thing causes me to feel like the sky is falling!

One problem that often accompanies negative emotion is the tendency to judge ourselves for having them. When I felt angry or depressed, I believed I was wrong to feel that way. My negative *thoughts* about my negative *emotions* compounded the problem. Negative emotions may be unpleasant to experience, but they're completely natural. Your emotions are valid regardless of what they are. Keep in mind that anger, sadness, anxiety, depression, and all the other negative emotions may provide important clues to aspects of yourself or you're your life that need changing or adjusting.

By focusing attention on the core issue, rather than on your negative emotions, you can solve issues directly. To do so, mentally step outside yourself and observe your emotions from a distance. Ask yourself, *"Why is this problem affecting me so much? Why does it bother me and bring these emotions? What is the core issue here, and how can I view it differently in order to feel better?"*

One suggestion is to separate your logical self from your emotional self. Use logic to remind yourself of all the great things in life and all the reasons you have to be happy. This may help control the negative emotions that are taking over and you'll be able to make a decision to be happy. Negative emotions do not last forever. Sometimes you just need to ride them out until they diminish, then attack them with positive thinking and affirmations. The key is to avoid allowing negative emotions to control you. If you have difficulty doing so and you experience deep depression or anxiety you cannot relieve, I recommend you seek professional help.

Serenity

Take time to smell the flowers. Mt. Elbert is the highest peak in Colorado and the second highest mountain in the contiguous United States. My mother climbed it at age 67 after meeting an experienced rock and mountain climber nine years her senior. He inspired her to join him, but because of her age, she was concerned her pace would be too slow.

As they hiked Mt. Elbert, they met and chatted briefly with a young couple climbing at a rapid pace. My mom and her friend finally reached the top and began a slow descent. When recounting the adventure, she described the beautiful flowers and the unusual rocks she had seen. They'd even encountered a buck. I wondered whether the young couple took time to enjoy the plants and wildlife. Both couples made the same climb, but I'm guessing only one couple enjoyed the beauty of the moment.

It's imperative to slow down and enjoy life. The old cliché, "It isn't about the destination, it's about the journey" is so true. Take your time. Slow down. Be present. Enjoy everything this world has to offer and you will see beauty and wonder popping up all around you.

Accept the past and present. An important aspect of serenity is letting go of the past. If you focus on the past, you open yourself to regret and shame, emotions that could bring lasting, negative feelings about yourself and others. Past experiences happened for a reason; they made you who you are today.

Being bullied in school made me more compassionate. Being a recovering drug addict and alcoholic taught me to be nonjudgmental about others fighting addiction or mental disorders. Perhaps I was destined to be an alcoholic who nearly died twice so I could help others face similar challenges. During my recovery, I learned to accept the horrible things I went through. Without them, I may not have hit my drunken, alcoholic bottom. And without hitting bottom, I may not have had the urgency or the will to recover. I am grateful for every experience, whether it was good, bad, or ugly.

When you feel unhappy about something in your past, acknowledge it. If someone else caused the problem, forgive them. If it was something you did, forgive yourself and vow to do better next time. Other than learning from your mistakes, there's no reason to spend time in the past. What's done is done and you can't change a single thing. Start with a clean slate. Harbor no shame or regret. Believe that everything that happened needed to happen for you to be the person you are today.

In addition to accepting the past, you must learn to accept any present situation that you can't change or leave. This may be especially difficult when you're strongly attached to a person or outcome, but practicing detachment is a good way to accept the present. One of my favorite sayings is, "It is what it is," because these words remind me to discharge the notion I'm attached to the problem. There is no sense worrying over something I can't change, so I must accept it. I can and must live with it. You can't make the sun shine on a rainy day, but you can learn to love dancing in the rain.

Forgive yourself and forgive others. Are you holding a grudge against someone? Is it the neighborhood kids who bullied you as a child or a co-worker who stole an idea? Perhaps you're holding a grudge against your parents for not providing enough love or a safe and nurturing home as you were growing up.

If you find yourself the target of someone's ill will, keep in mind they may act that way because they were a target of bullying themselves. If they act like a bully, they may have been bullied when they were younger by other children or maybe even their parents. As a result, that's what they know. That's what is comfortable for them. It doesn't make what they do right, but hopefully it makes it easier for you to understand and forgive their behavior.

Does this mean you should allow bad behavior directed at you to continue or that it's acceptable? Absolutely not. When you forgive someone, it doesn't mean what they did is appropriate. Forgiveness is for you, not for them. When you forgive someone, you set *yourself* free. As long as you carry negative feelings toward them, they remain in control. They have the power to make you feel a certain way—and the only person who should have that power is you.

Gratitude

Being grateful for what you have raises your vibration. Sometimes this may be difficult, I know. You may not have a perfect life or everything you've ever wanted, but others have less than you and feel content. Focus on the wonderful things in your life. Family and friends are a good start. You may not live in a fancy house, but you can be grateful you have a roof over your head. Your car may be a hoopty jalopy, but you can be grateful you don't have to ride the bus. There is something wonderful and unique about each of us, so be grateful and focus on the incredible being you are. No matter what your situation, you can be grateful for something in your life in order to raise your vibration.

*Once upon a time…*there was a small child too poor to have toys to play with. She found objects around the house and used her imagination as her playground. She put a blanket over chairs to create a "playhouse." She put dishes and silverware in her playhouse and made a small bed with a pillow. She took pots and pans, turned them upside down and pretended to be a drummer. She was happy playing this way because it was all she knew.

One day while walking to school, she found an old tattered doll on the side of the road. It looked as if it had been run over. It was dirty and the doll's dress was torn, but the little girl was overwhelmed with excitement! A toy! She treasured that doll for years.

The little girl who originally owned the doll lived in a wealthy household and received toys whenever she asked for them. On her birthday and at Christmas, her floor was covered with great gifts. She had received the doll several years ago as a Christmas gift. She opened it, played with it briefly then tossed it onto a heap of other toys. She rarely played with the doll and didn't value it because she had so many other toys to play with.

One doll cast aside by a little girl with everything; the same doll bringing years of happiness to another little girl who had nothing. Neither was happier than the other. The trick is being grateful for what you have now. It's wonderful to have goals and achieve them, but when you focus on things you don't have, or forget to be grateful for what you do have, you invite turmoil into your life. In truth, few of us need more things, we just need to be more grateful for what we already have. Then as we strive to have more and be more, we'll be happier along the journey.

It's all relative. I felt stressed a few years ago while planning a birthday party for my twins. I was overwhelmed and exhausted by ordering cakes, getting invitations out, preparing food, and everything else. Then the mother of my daughter's friend called to RSVP. I hadn't seen her since last year's birthday party so I asked how she was doing. "A lot better now," she said. When I asked what she meant, she told me she had developed breast cancer which resulted in a double mastectomy. Since the cancer was estrogen-driven, she also needed a hysterectomy. During the hysterectomy, her bladder was punctured which required her to carry a urostomy bag for weeks. Then there was the infection...

After hanging up, it struck me how ungrateful I was being. Other than a nagging case of insomnia, I had no health issues at all. A few days later, I saw her at the party and told her how happy and healthy she looked. I also told her she was an inspiration to her daughters—and to me.

Why do bad things happen? God is great. God is good. God is in your neighborhood. Why does God (or whatever your idea of him, her, or it may be) put us through these trials and tribulations? Why can't everyone on the planet be happy and healthy one hundred percent of the time? If that's what we wanted, we should have stayed in heaven (or whatever you call the great beyond). I believe we came here to gain experiences, to learn, and to discover who we really are. I also believe we're here to advance our souls and that requires some hard lessons to knock us for a loop.

Everybody suffers tough times. Struggle is part of life. You can either allow bad times to make you bitter and angry (which creates more things to be bitter or angry about), or you can view tough breaks as character-building experiences. Only the second option helps you achieve a pleasant state of mind.

Who do you believe has better coping mechanisms—a person who enjoyed an easy life or the one who triumphed over tough times? Difficulty teaches us what really matters. It provides insight into who we are, builds our character, and teaches us the importance of loving ourselves and others. Difficult times happen for a reason, so take the opportunity to learn everything you can from them. As someone who survived tough times, I am grateful for them. They made me into the person I am today...and I wouldn't have it any other way.

Good times are like chocolate cake. If you only experience good times, you won't have anything to compare them with. Imagine that we all lead perfect lives. We're all beautiful or handsome and we all have more money than we dreamed of. Undoubtedly, we would be shallow, spoiled human beings who never learned the important—but tough—lessons. It would be difficult for emotional, mental, and spiritual growth to occur. Plus, the world would be very boring!

Look at it like chocolate cake. If chocolate cake were the only food on planet Earth, we would quickly get sick of eating it for breakfast, lunch, and dinner. And, if chocolate cake was all we had, we couldn't compare it to brussels sprouts or liver. We wouldn't know how delicious it is because there would be nothing to compare it with.

"Mom, what's for dinner?"

"Chocolate cake."

"Chocolate cake again? Yuck!"

Instead, we have a huge selection of foods to choose from, so chocolate cake is only enjoyed on rare occasions. Without brussels sprouts and liver, we can't fully appreciate how wonderful chocolate cake is. Likewise, without the bad things that happen, we wouldn't fully appreciate and be grateful for the good things.

Hospital Stay. Woe is me! How could this happen? I awakened in the middle of the night with a severe pain in my abdomen. I told myself, "You're tough, suck it up." Two hours later, I couldn't take the pain anymore. After looking up the symptoms online (never do that!), I was convinced I was having a gallbladder attack. I was hoping for immediate surgery so I would never have to go through that pain again.

At 3:30 a.m., the emergency room doctor poked and prodded, then ordered an EKG, x-rays, blood tests, a CAT scan, and every other test developed by modern medicine. Five hours later, the doctor approached me with a puzzled look on his face. "We can't find anything wrong with you," he said. "Here are a couple of prescriptions. There's a pharmacy at the other end of the hospital. You're free to go."

Given the severity of the pain, it was difficult to believe he couldn't diagnose what was wrong. I searched for the pharmacy and finally found it—it was closed. I gingerly made my way back across the hospital to my car, bent over in debilitating pain.

Weeks later, the physical pain was gone, but I suffered emotional pain over the bill I received. The total cost for my five-hour stay in the ER was $15,979, and $5,000 of it was my responsibility. Even worse was the fact that only two months prior to my hospital visit, I cancelled my "Cadillac" health insurance plan featuring a low deductible. I opted for a cheaper plan since *I never go to the doctor or hospital*. My alimony had ended and I thought I could save money. I felt very sorry for myself until I realized the date was September 11.

Thousands of people lost their lives on September 11, 2001 only because they happened to be in the wrong place at the wrong time. Thousands more lost friends or loved ones. The money for my hospital visit no longer seemed like a huge issue and my self-pity disintegrated. I was alive and healthy. When you maintain a proper perspective, the path to gratitude is near at hand.

STEP TWELVE – SUMMARY AND WORKSHOP

✓ Emotions vibrate at a certain frequency and the universe will align your reality to that same frequency.

✓ Become and remain an observer of your emotions. Align your emotions to those you would have if you were already your best self, living your dream life.

✓ Negative feelings can sabotage the creative process.

✓ Be content with the way you are, everything you have, and your life as it exists now.

✓ Every minute spent sad or angry is a minute you cannot get back.

✓ If you expect outside sources to make you happy, you will never be happy. "If only I had this" or "If only that would happen" should never be followed by "then I'd be happy."

✓ Positive emotions come from love. Negative emotions come from fear. Unfortunately, fear often comes disguised as love.

✓ Switching from a fear-based reaction to a love-based reaction will shift you into a higher vibration.

✓ When you desire something, think of it as a preference rather than a requirement (which if not met, makes you unhappy).

✓ Separate yourself from your emotions. Use logic to remind yourself there are many things to be happy about.

✓ Ride out negative emotions until they're not so overwhelming, then attack them with positive thoughts and affirmations.

✓ Don't be afraid of your emotions. When you know your feelings are valid, they lose their power to affect you as much.

✓ Everything you need to create happiness lies within you. You are complete. You are enough.

✓ Enjoy life's journey. Take your time. Slow down. Stay in the present. Enjoy everything the moment has to offer and you will see beauty and wonder popping up all around you.

✓ All your experiences happened for a reason and made you who you are. Other than visiting your past to learn from mistakes, there is no reason to spend time there.

✓ You can't make the sun shine on a rainy day, but you can learn to love dancing in the rain.

✓ Worrying about the future doesn't make it better, it only takes away your serenity.

✓ Right now—*this second*—are you having an immediate problem? If the answer is no, then stop worrying! If the answer is yes, then fix the problem or accept it.

✓ When you forgive someone, you set yourself free. Forgiveness is for you, not for them.

✓ When you resent someone who wronged you, that person retains their control over you. You allow them to make you feel a certain way, and the only person who should have that power is you.

✓ Always feel grateful. It raises your vibration and enables the universe to help manifest your dreams.

✓ Who has better coping skills, the person living an easy life, or the person who had to prevail over many trials and tribulations?

✓ Difficult times teach you what really matters. The challenges you face provide insight into who you are, build your character, and teach you the importance of loving yourself. They show how much strength and courage you really have.

Happiness

_____ Under any circumstance you can concentrate on the most positive aspect of a situation. For example, let's say a recent plumbing leak cost you $1,000 to repair. Instead of focusing on the money, focus on the fact you now have new plumbing in part of your home. Perhaps you have a sick friend or family member. Instead of focusing on the tragedy of the sickness, focus on the fact you're becoming closer and experiencing more love than you would have under normal circumstances. It won't change the severity of the situation, but it will change how you look at it. More importantly, it changes your vibration. Not only does this benefit you, it benefits the people around you, including your friend who is ill. You may not be able to change the circumstance that's making you unhappy; but you can focus on the best possible aspect of the situation in order to raise your vibration so you're not creating more unhappiness.

_____ Examine each goal, one at a time, and think about how you would feel if that goal were realized. Feeling the emotions you would feel if your goals have already been achieved will raise your vibration, making it easier for the universe to help manifest them.

_____ Use emotions to raise your vibration. Sometimes it helps to use a previous situation. For example, if the goal is to make more friends, recall a time when you made a new friend and then use your imagination to amplify the feelings of happiness and acceptance you felt. If your goal is to have more money, think back to receiving a bonus or having a good month financially. If you felt successful and secure, use your imagination to focus on those feelings. If your goal is to own a BMW, imagine how ecstatic you were when you bought your very first car. Use your imagination to amplify that same feeling.

You can also focus on something that brings you that emotion now. If your goal is to become healthier, think how grateful you are for eyes with which to see, or legs which carry you from room to room. Bask in this gratitude until it becomes easier to imagine feeling this way about your whole physical state. This raises your vibration and makes good health easier to attain.

_____ Decide to be happy. Imagine you're 85 years old looking back on your life. Will you wish you'd been happier during your time on this planet? Will you look back and think you did the best you could to live every day to its fullest? Did you try your best to lead a happy, fulfilling life? If not, now is the time to create more happiness worth remembering. Why waste your life being unhappy?

_____ Every morning right after you wake, say to yourself, "It's a great day. I'm in a good mood. I'm happy." Start the day being proactive about your feelings. Decide you're happy and decide you'll focus on the positive aspects of the day instead of dwelling on the negative. Don't allow outside situations or other people to influence your mood. You have more power than you may think.

_____ * Write down ten things you can do that will make you happy. Is it roller skating? Going to the movies? Eating out? Treating yourself to a manicure? Schedule time each week to engage in an activity that makes you feel happy.

_____ Focus on the people, places, and things that make you feel happy. Instead of fretting about the horrible life you lead, concentrate on the wonderful things you already have and the accomplishments that lie ahead. Focus on the good you see in the world. You have the ability to place your focus wherever you decide.

_____ Think of someone who rubs you the wrong way. Is it a friend, a family member, or a co-worker? Do they bicker with you or tell stories about you behind your back? Are you caught up in the drama? Do you argue or gossip about them? You may be expressing fear that you'll lose the argument or look bad to others. You may also be worried you truly are as they see you, or maybe you're just mad at the gall this person has. It's important to handle such situations carefully.

Instead of arguing, look at him or her and think, "It's okay they feel that way. We will simply agree to disagree." There are over seven billion people on the planet. It's logical to assume some of them won't agree with you and won't like you. You *can't* control that. What you *can* control is your reaction to them. Instead of taking revenge by continuing to argue or gossip, take the high road. People will respect you for it and may see the other person for who they really are. Most importantly, you will increase your respect for yourself and lessen the impact the other person has on you.

To take this a step further, imagine yourself coming from a place of **love** instead of **fear.** You can prevent others from sucking the happiness out of you and you won't feel the need to retaliate. In order to accomplish this, bless these people with love in your prayers, meditation, and/or thoughts. Instead of engaging in their drama, imagine them living a life of joy and happiness. Each day, before you encounter people you don't get along with, imagine them this way. Find a way to genuinely wish them happiness. *This may be difficult* and you may need to spend some time working on the best way to achieve it; but if you come from a place of love, the fear this person created in you will dissipate.

When I first tried this, I experienced a totally foreign feeling. I believe it was my vibration rising in response to my thoughts of compassion for my adversary. Once you are able to wish the best for problematic people in your life, you start to become free of their ability to cause you to feel negatively.

_____ * Write letters in your notebook to people with whom you're having problems. Don't actually mail these letters; they're just a tool to explore your thoughts and feelings. Tell your side of the story from beginning to end, including how the other person hurt you. Include as many details as you can. It's fine to fill the letter with negativity. Be perfectly honest and let it all hang out. *Be very careful, however, that it isn't seen or read by others.* Once you've expressed yourself with no holds barred, write a second letter that is more diplomatic. Then write another. You'll find yourself being less emotional as you write letter after letter. I have written as many as six letters and by the sixth, my emotions were much calmer. In fact, if the other person were to read the final version, it wouldn't shock them like the first. I never send the notes, but I find it validating to put my thoughts in writing. I can read the letter, analyze it, and see whether I'm being overly dramatic (from a passing mood) or justified in my feelings. This exercise can be calming as well as healing.

_____Stop the "if-only-isms." If you look for outside sources of happiness, you will be embarking on a frustrating, never-ending question. "If only I had this" or "If only that would happen" should never be followed by "then I'd be happy. Wipe these notions out of your mind. If you do, you will be happier in every moment.

_____ To be happy, use your imagination. You've probably heard that the simple act of smiling makes you feel happy. You can't feel unhappy when you're smiling, right? Take this a step further and use your creativity to *imagine* you're happy. What does that feel like? When you can imagine happiness for a few seconds, extend that to a few minutes. Soon you'll be able to turn it on like a switch.

_____ Anxiety makes the brightest day seem glum. If you experience light headedness, a fast heart rate, racing thoughts, extreme worry, trembling, tightening in the chest, or you find yourself obsessing over a particular concern, you may have a problem with anxiety. Step outside the anxiety and the problem causing it. Be an observer of your emotions.

Imagine your anxiety as a ball of energy, totally separate and distinct from yourself. Visualize it leaving your body and floating alongside your head (mine always floats on my left side for some reason). Now visualize this mass breaking into millions of pieces and dispersing harmlessly into the universe. It helps to say to the mass (yes, talk to the mass), "You are not real. You are separate from me. I am peaceful and calm, so you can go now."

Immediately imagine feeling peaceful and calm. The more you practice this exercise, the easier it will be to master your anxiety.

_____ Focus your attention on the anxiety and seek where it's manifesting in your body. I feel mine in my chest and throat. Both areas feel tight and it feels as if I could hyperventilate. You may be different, so pay attention to your body when you're anxious, so you can help alleviate the discomfort. Imagine a calming sensation pouring over this place in your body. Try envisioning a white or yellow light or a warm and soothing energy surpassing your anxious sensations. I've even visualized warm, smooth honey flowing through my chest and throat and successfully alleviated the anxiety.

_____ Calm breathing exercises can help with anxiety. Sometimes anxiety causes us to have shallow breaths from the upper part of the chest making the upper chest expand. Try breathing deep breaths from your belly and make sure you exhale fully. You know you're doing this correctly when your abdomen expands. Then close your eyes and recite this affirmation: I breathe in calmness and I breathe out anxiety. Doing this exercise can cut down your anxiety tremendously.

_____ When you feel anxious, go outside and take a walk or go to another room. A change of scenery will help your mind focus on something different.

Serenity

_____ Serenity is found by noticing the beauty and wonder around you. As you improve your observational skills, you'll find calmness and tranquility in everyday activities. Look around the room right now and find something beautiful. Maybe it's flowers in a vase or art on the wall. Possibly, it's the way a blanket is draped over a chair or maybe it's the curves in a couch. Is someone else in the room? It could be the twinkle in a friend's eye or a smile of happiness. Our surroundings can usually offer something of beauty to appreciate if we look hard enough.

_____ Practice mindfulness for five minutes. Stop everything and focus on the awareness you have of your body and surroundings. Notice how your clothing or the furniture feels against your skin. Notice how the room smells or how the warmth of your body radiates outward. This exercise will get you out of your head and into your body. It will also help alleviate worrying about a future event or regretting a past event by placing your focus on the present moment. Worry will fade away and serenity will take its place.

_____ If you're dreading a task, but you're already committed, it helps to reward yourself after completing the task. Perhaps you made a promise to help someone move across town or help paint a friend's basement. You don't feel up to the task, but it's too late to back out. Try planning something afterward as a reward. Take yourself out for ice cream, get a pedicure, or see a movie. Then when you're doing the task you can have the reward in the back of your mind as something to look forward to. The point is to find serenity in every situation no matter how daunting it may be.

_____ * List ten activities that could help you feel serene. Set aside 20 minutes each day to do something from that list. If there's a park near your home, you could take your dog for a walk (without your cell phone). Take a nap, read a book, write a journal, ride a bike, take a bath, meditate, cook, or listen to soft music. Do something—anything—to feel serene.

_____ Accept the past. Are you haunted by something that happened in your past? Is it something you've done or said? You should acknowledge it, forgive yourself, and move on. Did something bad happen to you or someone you love? Does it help to wallow in negative emotions from a past event? No. Does it make you happy or sad to do this? Other than learning from the past, there's no reason to spend time there. *The past is set in stone. Your thoughts about the past are not. The present moment and the future are not.* Work on what can be changed instead of focusing on what cannot.

_____ When you feel negative emotions about a situation, replace your thoughts with the command word, "Detach." Picture the problem as a bubble floating in front of you. As you're repeating the command word "detach" imagine the bubble slowly floating away. Imagine a feeling of detachment from the problem as if it is completely separate from you. Keep telling yourself, "Detach...detach...detach....."

_____ Is there an upcoming event that jeopardizes your serenity? Ask yourself, "What's the worst thing that can happen?" If you have to speak in public, you may be concerned you'll misspeak or forget your words. Will the audience laugh at you? Will you ever see them again? Does it really matter what they think? In most situations you face, the worst possible outcome is far less damaging than what you imagine. When things turn out better than you feared, you'll be that much happier. Don't ruin the present by worrying about something in the future. The threat of unhappiness lies in your fear, not in the problem itself.

_____ * Make a list of everyone who hurt you that you've been unable to forgive. The list may include people who were mean to you or abandoned you. It may include people who stole from you or cheated on you. Next to their names, write what they did to cause such anger and resentment. Now, one at a time, imagine them sitting in a chair in front of you. Recall what they did and think about what you want to say to them.

It's okay to let out your feelings! When I did this exercise, I screamed every four-letter word I knew at the top of my lungs! This exercise helped purge my negative thoughts about two individuals who fueled my downward spiral beginning in the seventh grade. Afterwards, I felt free. Even though I only imagined them in front of me, I left nothing unsaid. Within minutes, I released my resentment and turned my attention to finding forgiveness. Maybe their parents treated them badly in childhood. Perhaps they developed so much self-loathing they chose to lash out at me. This doesn't make what they did acceptable, but it helped me get past what they did.

After completing this exercise, not only did I forgive them, I genuinely wished them contentment and joy. Releasing my anger by imagining them in front of me validated my feelings and allowed me to focus on healing. Holding onto or denying feelings only makes things worse.

_____ * Write down why people do or say hurtful things. Maybe the person just broke up with his or her significant other. They might have been up all night with a sick relative. Were they just fired? Were they bullied and made fun of when they were children? Did they come from troubled homes? Maybe the person is just a miserable human being. When someone said or did something that hurt, one of these reasons may explain why. It may not have been anything you said or did. This doesn't excuse their behavior, of course, but it will remind you that they have the problem—not you. Whatever the reason, is there a way you could find a smidgeon of forgiveness in your heart? Even a small bit of forgiveness can help you have a more positive mindset. Don't take things people say or do personally. They might be lashing out because of something that has nothing to do with you.

_____ * Can you imagine the people who hurt you living a life of joy and happiness? Each day, before you encounter people you don't get along with, imagine them this way. Don't engage in their drama. Focus on the love you have for yourself and find a way to genuinely wish them happiness. Once you wish others well, you become free. Forgiveness isn't for them, it's for you.

Gratitude

_____ Right now, look up from this book at objects or people in the room. Pick just one thing for which you are grateful. Is it a painting on the wall that gives you pleasure? Is it your dog lying next to you on the couch? Is it the leafy trees outside the window? Select something and focus on the good feelings it gives you; then choose something else, then pick another. Can you feel your emotional state change? That's you vibrating at a higher frequency. Continue this feeling of gratitude throughout the day and the results will be amplified. There is always something nearby for which to be grateful. Stop and focus on it. This exercise will increase your vibration and allow the universe to bring you a reality that aligns with that higher vibration.

_____ * In your notebook, list everything you can think of that causes you to feel grateful. If you have a difficult time deciding what should go on your list, expand your mind a bit. If you're grateful for your TV, that's fine. Put it on the list. You could even include the TV works, the TV is big enough to see clearly, the TV is loud enough, or the TV is great entertainment. There are infinite possibilities for your list. Read the list and bask in the gratitude for a few moments.

_____ * Take a look at your list and imagine everything NOT listed will disappear in five minutes. Now add whatever you don't want to lose. The list may double or triple in length, and the exercise could take a very long time. Consider things like running water, a roof over your head, family members, friends, your computer, and all the other things you use or enjoy daily.

_____ * Every night before you go to bed, list three things for which you're grateful. It's okay to duplicate items from the list you just made. Reminding yourself of important things raises your awareness of the pleasures in life. If you list someone you love, think about what you most love about them. Focus on everything about that person that causes you to feel grateful. If it's your house, focus on the fact it gives you shelter. Even if your car is a beater, you can be grateful you have transportation. Add to your list each night and I promise your gratitude will raise your vibration and make it easier for the universe to create even more things that cause you to feel grateful.

_____ To help remind you to be grateful, put something unique in your pocket, or wear a ring, or put a piece of tape on your finger. Each time you see that little reminder, think about something in your life for which you're grateful.

_____ Put a sticky note with affirmations on your bathroom mirror. The note should say, "I am grateful for _____." Fill in the blank with the top three things that cause you to feel grateful. Recite the affirmation every time you look in the mirror and focus on the feeling of gratitude.

PART III—CONCLUSION

I have sometimes wondered, "Where is the world taking me?" I wondered because my life was largely controlled by addictive substances, outside influences, and my subconscious running amok. I lived life by default, not by design. The process of creating "me" and my life was moving forward every second of every day, but I wasn't the one in control. I finally realized I could set and achieve worthy goals, not only by breaking them into smaller pieces and actively working on them, but by speaking, thinking, acting, and feeling as if they were already a reality.

Is life all you want it to be? Are you reaching your full potential and creating your best self? What would your thoughts, words, actions, and emotions be if you were already the person you wanted to be and already lived the life of your dreams? You *can* get there from here!

When your thoughts don't align with a newer, better version of yourself, change your thoughts. When your words don't sound like your best self, change your words. When you do something your best self would never do, make a promise never to do it again. When negative emotions seem to envelope you, focus on the most positive thing in your world at that moment. Make a conscious effort to imagine your best self and your dream life, and then act as if that was your reality.

Remember, every thought, word, action, and emotion you have vibrates at a certain frequency and the universe responds with consequences that match your vibration. Align your frequency with the reality you wish to have and the person you wish to be. Raise your vibration and enable the universe to manifest good things in your life. Do you wonder where life is taking you? It's time to see yourself as the source of what happens in life, not its victim. Take charge and create your own future.

PART III – SUGGESTED READING

The Magic Lamp: Goal Setting for People Who Hate Setting Goals by Keith Ellis (New York: Three Rivers Press, 1998).

How to Set Goals: Your Goal Setting Bible for Maximum Personal Achievement by Darrin Wiggins (CreateSpace Independent Publishing Platform, 2013).

Life by Design: 6 Steps to an Extraordinary You by Tom Ferry (New York: Ballantine Books, 2010).

The Field: The Quest for the Secret Force of the Universe by Lynne McTaggart (New York: HarperCollins Publishers, 2002).

Spiritual Growth: Being Your Higher Self by Sanaya Roman (Tiburon, CA: HJ Kramer Inc., 1989).

The Secret by Rhonda Byrne (Hillsboro, OR: Atria Books, 2006). *Wherever You Go There You Are: Mindfulness Meditations* by John Kabat-Zinn (New York: Hyperion, 2005).

Meditation for Beginners by Jack Kornfield (Boulder, CO: Sounds True, Inc., 2008).

Ask and It Is Given: Learning to Manifest Your Desires by Esther and Jerry Hicks (Carlsbad, CA: Hay House, Inc., 2004).

The Hidden Messages in Water by Masaru Emoto (Hillsboro, OR: Beyond Words Publishing, Inc., 2004).

A Complaint Free World: How to Stop Complaining and Start Enjoying the Life You Always Wanted by Will Bowen (New York: Doubleday, 2007).

Who Moved My Cheese? An Amazing Way to Deal with Change in Your Work and in Your Life by Spencer Johnson (New York: G.P. Putnam's Sons, 2002).

Your Road Map to Lifelong Happiness: A Guide to the Life You Want by Ken Keyes, Jr. (Coos Bay, OR: Love Line Books, 1995).

Your Life is a Gift: So Make the Most of it! by Ken Keyes, Jr. (Coos Bay, OR: Love Line Books, 1987).

Conversations With God: An Uncommon Dialogue by Neal Donald Walsch (New York: G. P. Putnam's Sons, 1995).

Attitude is Everything by Keith Harrell (New York: HarperCollins Publishers Inc., 2003).

The Joy Compass: 8 Ways to Find Lasting Happiness & Optimism in the Present Moment by Donald Altman Maler (Oakland, CA: New Harbinger Publications, 2012).

The Power of Now: A Guide to Spiritual Enlightenment by Eckhart Tolle (Novato, CA: New World Library, 1999).

Chicken Soup for the Soul: The Power of Forgiveness by Amy Newmark and Anthony Anderson (Cos Cob, CT: Chicken Soup for the Soul Publishing, LLC 2014).

FINAL CONCLUSION

What's that noise?

It's the sound of victory! Sometimes you win; sometimes you lose. The trick is to always keep your head high, keep reaching for the stars, and maintain a winning attitude. Before he invented the light bulb, Thomas Edison said, "I have not failed. I've just found 10,000 ways that will not work."

Stay consistent in your effort to remain clean and sober, heal yourself, and create the life you desire. A balloon filled with helium doesn't stay in the air forever. Before long, the helium seeps out and the balloon sinks to the floor. For it to remain airborne, it needs an occasional infusion of new helium. The same applies to your sobriety. Self-healing and creating a new life also need regular attention or you could fall back into the rut you fought so hard to escape.

Marathon runners train for many months before a race; their dedication is unwavering. Can you put the needed perseverance into improving your inner self and your outlook on life? Can you take just 15 minutes each day to quiet your mind and recite positive affirmations of who you want to be? Can you spare ten minutes to re-read one of the chapters in this book and complete a few workshop items? Yes, you can. The minimal effort you put into healing yourself will return great rewards.

While the steps I outline in this book aren't difficult, they do require time and commitment. This isn't a book you read once and say, "Aha! I got it," then never read again. Develop a routine to practice one step each week and commit to that step *every day of that week*. Where affirmations are suggested, do them every day that week. Pick a chapter and re-read it every day for a week. Once the steps become second nature, you'll feel the changes growing within you.

I hope you experience the total transformation I achieved. I went from a shy, introverted, shell of a person into a confident, carefree, fun-loving individual who loves life. It didn't happen overnight. It took several years of self-reflection, hard work, and open-minded willingness to seek answers. I wrote this book to help you face similar problems, so you have a "cheat sheet" to consult. Hopefully your transformation won't be as difficult or take as long as mine.

At this point, not only do I have a better awareness of who I am, I've also created a higher version of myself. I have friends and family with whom I share mutual love and respect. I engage in healthy, productive activities that boost my self-confidence. It's okay for me to think and feel what comes naturally. I no longer need to hide my true self, my thoughts, or my feelings. I am perfect just the way I am.

You can also change yourself into someone who doesn't require addictive substances or destructive behavior to cope with each coming day. There is a better life for you. Start today. You're worth it!

Thoughts, words, actions, and emotions vibrate at certain frequencies. The universe picks up on those frequencies and brings forth a reality that matches. To create a better version of yourself and the life you desire, be an observer of your thoughts, words, actions, and emotions. Align them to those you would have if you were already the person you want to be, living the life of your dreams. Remember, even when you're not intentionally creating yourself and your life, they are being created by default.

ABOUT THE AUTHOR

After struggling with addiction for many years, April Aimee Adams turned her life around. She graduated summa cum laude with a bachelor's degree in psychology in 2009. Owner of Rodnee Books, LLC, she has published four inspirational books. Her main goal in life is to help people create positive mindsets, be the best they can be, and live life by design, not by default. To learn more go to aaaworkshops.com.

A note from the author:

To my amazing readers: My goal is to help as many people as I can with my books and workshops. If you found any part of this book helpful and you think others would benefit from it, please take a few moments and leave a review on.Amazon.com. Every review is helpful. Thank you so much!

Also by April Aimee Adams:

That Don't Make Ya Bad: A Memoir of Addiction
*Ebook available on Amazon
Paperback available at aaaworkshops.com

The Law of Attraction in Action: Five Steps to Making the Law of Attraction Work for You
*Available on Amazon

21755596R00107

Made in the USA
San Bernardino, CA
05 January 2019